ORIENT-EXPRESS
HOTELS

PARIS
REVISITED

ALISON CULLIFORD

DEDICATION

To Matthew Whyte,
for introducing me to Paris.

"WHAT IS MOST BEAUTIFUL ABOUT HER IS NEITHER NOTRE-DAME NOR ANY OTHER EDIFICE, IT IS PARIS HERSELF."

JULES MICHELET,
FRENCH HISTORIAN (1798-1874)

LVTETIA, vulgari nomine Paris, vrbs
Galliæ maxima, Sequana nauigabili flu-
mine irrigatur, nobili gente, mercator, fre-
quentia vniuersitate excellenti, stupendi
operis templo B. Mariæ, Palatio Regio, alijs
que præstantissimis ædificijs, tribunali
æquissimorum Iudicum, & pulcherrimis
epitaphijs, florentissima ✿ ✿ ✿

PARIS pour vray eft la maifo royalle, Inde en eftude, & en poetes Romme, Fecunde en vin, &c.
Du dieu Phœbus en splendeur radiale Athenes lors en malic trefscauat homme. Fertile en bled, & c
Ceſt Cyrrhea pleine de bons efpritz, Roſier mondain, heauline du firmament,
Trefheureux faiſans diuers eſcriptz Vniuerſel, de Sidon lornemene
Ceſt Chryſea en metaulx habondante Tres habondante en viures et breuuaiges,
Grece de pris en leurs floriſſantc Riche en beaulx champs & fiuneux riuages

CONTE

PREFA

At Orient-Express, our guests often ask us to share our secrets about the cities in which we live and work, or even just the ones we love. So when the opportunity arose to be involved with a series of books celebrating some of our favourite cities and their 'spirit of place' we were delighted to join in.

C E

Such books can never be comprehensive; many places or experiences that are featured in every guidebook may well have been left out. But in their place are some insights, special glimpses that may not have been seen before. What we are talking about here is the joy of discovery which cities like Paris, Venice, London or Florence can still offer, if you know where to look, over and over and over again.

I think it was the late, great humorist and broadcaster Frank Muir who sighed, "Ah Paris, where only the river is sane". We can only agree, no city has quite the romantic appeal of Paris. It was from here that the famous journey undertaken by the original Orient-Express back in 1883 began, on its way to the legendary city of Constantinople, now Istanbul. It is a trip which we recreate, in all its classic splendour, once every year in August. And, of course, many of our guests spend a few days in Paris before joining the Venice Simplon-Orient-Express on its journey to and from Venice.

In her own discovery of Paris, the author, Alison Culliford, made many stops on the way, all of which are listed in the back of the book. Finding one's way around Paris is never easy, but as getting lost is a prerequisite to getting to know a city of style, this is simply a bonus. We hope you enjoy the experience.

SIMON SHERWOOD
President, Orient-Express Hotels

WHAT MAKES

"There's something about Paris that always makes

THRILLING?

PARIS SO

me feel fairly full of *espièglerie* and *joie de vivre*",

muses Bertie Wooster, preparing for a jaunt across the Channel
in *Carry On, Jeeves*. We may not express it in such chipper
terms, but there aren't many people who could claim to be
unmoved by the prospect of a few days, a few weeks or even
a lifetime in this enchanting city.

What is it about Paris that makes the mere idea of it send
tingles down the spine? How can a single word, derived from
the name of a rather grubby marsh-dwelling tribe, evoke such
visions of splendour? Of course Paris has majestic architecture,
wickedly indulgent food, gorgeous shop windows and a vibrant
night life. Its reputation floats on a raft of images – of sparkling
lights around the Élysées, platters of seafood borne aloft by
suited waiters, elegant mannequins sporting the New Look,
absinthe-fuelled nights of gay abandon. But more than all
these, Paris has a spirit that takes it right through to the
present – in a word, optimism.

This optimism is written all over the city. As you stride down
a grandiose avenue or take in the almost too picture-perfect
streets of the Left Bank or the Île de la Cité, it's easy to forget
that Paris has had a decidedly rocky ride. In the 1870s Thomas
Cook took the first war tourists to see ruined Paris. One can
only imagine the brightly attired ladies and behatted gentlemen
picking their way through the rubble caused by the "Terrible
Year" when the Prussian seige was followed by Communard
uprising. What did Paris do? It set to, rebuilding itself as an

even more glorious capital and held an exhibition to display itself to the world. The 1878 Exhibition unveiled the Sacré-Coeur, a great white edifice that proclaimed Paris a new Constantinople. 1889, the centenary of the Revolution, gave us the Eiffel Tower, a monument that spoke not only of patriotism but of modernity – a chance to say "Ya-boo" to the world. And the world adored it, just as it does today.

In the last century's upheavals what Paris was spared architecturally it suffered spiritually. Hitler thought the city so beautiful that he could bear to spare it only if the new Berlin surpassed it. Meanwhile Paris' pride kept *haute couture* in its rightful home, kept resistance member and adopted French citizen Josephine Baker singing, kept Sartre and Camus writing and gave a blind beggar the courage to play 'The Marseillaise' on his accordion. After the Libération, fashion flourished in defiant folds of fabric, cuisine reached new heights instead of allowing itself to be debased by the effects of rationing, and the spirit of liberation allowed a new youth culture to evolve. In the later years of the 20th century Paris was enriched by new cultural influences – though not without their conflicts – while culturally and architecturally a strong avant-garde vein continues to break through the famous Parisian conservatism.

Paris is a city in love with its own myths. Everywhere there are statues, to kings, emperors, revolutionaries and even mere ideas, such as liberty or dance. Charles de Gaulle is the latest to be immortalized – his swinging-hipped figure now sashays down the Champs-Élysées, despite his own wishes to the contrary – while 2001 saw the Bastille lit up by fireworks in honour of François Mitterrand. But Paris is deeply romantic, incurably nostalgic. Think of Napoléon, exiled in disgrace in 1815, his remains brought back for a state funeral sponsored by the restored monarchy in 1840. More recently, the *événements* of '68 have acquired a mythology of their own, and members of the litterati, not to mention the present-day establishment, are fondly referred to as *soixante-huitards*.

This curious trait can illuminate all sorts of intriguing corners and aspects of Paris. The lost river Bièvre, covered over when it became horribly polluted, is now the focus of as many as 50 societies trying to get it flowing through the city again. Foreign artists and musicians who chose Paris as their home, such as Chopin, Maria Callas or the Egyptian diva Dalida, have their graves showered with fresh flowers. Even restaurants are taken to people's hearts. 1998 saw a much publicized battle between *Les Amis du Balzar* (numbering a not unsubstantial 500) and the brasserie's new owner, who had taken certain items off the menu. Nostalgia and devotion to a *cause célèbre*, however bizarre or marginal, are daily rituals of Paris life. But then, where but in France would you find whole fraternities dedicated to the preservation of the *tarte Tatin*, or, indeed, mayonnaise?

Food, food, food. You could happily eat your way through Paris' 20 arrondissements (districts) and still want more. Paris is celebrated as the gastronomic capital of the world, but the cooking is still surprisingly close to the *terroir*. It doesn't take much to get a chef talking about maman's apple tart and even the hautest of *haute cuisine* pays real homage to the traditions of a region. Brasseries, that most Parisian institution, still serve extravagant portions of Alsatian food in Belle Époque surroundings, while bistros are where you'll find hearty south-western specialities. At the markets, food comes into the city still caked with a little country soil, or, from further afield, with the potent smells of herbs and spices enlivened by strong North African accents.

Paris is a sensory city. A sweet confection wrapped in tissue paper, it holds intense joys under tinselly wrapping. There is the joy of shopping, window or otherwise, in a city where everything is dressed to impress, from couture to croissants. Residents, accustomed to the daily fripperies, may well laugh when a visitor emerges from the boulangerie with a look of astonishment, saying, "Look, they did this" and proffering a perfect, one-person strawberry tart wrapped in a pyramid of paper.

Paris' smells and tastes are surprisingly strong for a northern city. Michael Palin rather winsomely describes the Métro as smelling of caramel. More enticing is the fact that a morning walk down a shop-lined street exudes the smell of cheeses and freshly baked bread, oranges and flowers which all spill out from the shopfronts. *Dégustations* are proffered wherever you go – slivers of the darkest chocolate, grapes and dates slipped into your fruit purchases to tempt you, samples of cheese from every area, dark and potent sips of wine, along with their long and varied histories. This is the way to learn about food and wine – on the street, one link away from their origins. Perhaps the most Parisian smell is that of the *tabac*, a mixture of heady tobacco smoke, newspapers and the aroma of espresso. More exotically, at dinner in the garden of the Mosquée, small posies of jasmine are sold for perfuming drawers, and their scent floats across the air long before the vendor comes into view.

Visiting Paris leaves you with flashes of vision in a moving city: ghostly Sacré-Coeur, illuminated by shafts of light through the rainclouds as you sweep through the overland stations of line 2 of the Métro; rollerblading policemen with hands clasped dapperly behind their backs; dancing figures through the window of a restaurant after midnight; children's windmills on a Haussmannian balcony; the gypsy chanteuse who sweeps by to the next station leaving a haunting echo of her song and a little boy waving...

Paris is never static, least of all in terms of which area is currently in the spotlight. Take Montmartre: a year or so ago you might have thought it was beyond redemption; but the films *Amélie Poulain* and *Moulin Rouge* have engendered a new love for the *Butte*. The Élysées are also enjoying a revival of popularity, once again attracting the smart set to hip new bars and restaurants cheek by jowl with hackneyed tourist haunts. The old wine warehouses of Bercy have been converted into bars, shops and cinemas; open-air jazz and cinema fill the site of the former city abattoirs at La Villette; and artists have colonized the industrial wasteland of the 13th arrondissement and Ménilmontant, which is where you can find the spirit of the old Montmartre and Montparnasse. Paris is also vibrantly multicultural. Rai and African beats are now the music of Paris, *tagine* and *teriyaki* are on the menu, and the streets of the north-east are enlivened by the colours and patterns of West Africa.

As you encircle the Périphérique by car in the early hours of the morning, it sometimes feels as though you could hold Paris in the palm of your hand. Circling the city you can actually see the Eiffel Tower, the Église de Sacré-Coeur and the tower of Montparnasse, tiny like models on an architect's 3-D plan. Spiral ever inwards through the snail's shell of arrondissements and eventually you are at the medieval centre, the Île de la Cité. But what is Paris' heart? Is it magnificent Notre-Dame, connected by the aching arms of two bridges? Is it the foreboding Palais de Justice? Or, a far more pleasing thought, could Paris' heart actually be Berthillon, the ice cream shop on the Île St-Louis?

Beyond the gleaming monuments it is the detail of Paris that entrances, and there is no better way to see it than on foot. Few cities are as kind to the walker as Paris. The city is compact, human in scale, and it has a beauty that alters with every change of light. In a glinting dawn Liberty takes flight from its column at the Bastille; Notre-Dame broods; pigeons perch on the Vendôme column before the jewellers have opened their doors. There are the unsuspected sights that only the walker sees: the glimpse of greenery down an artisans' passageway in the Faubourg St-Antoine; the frail old lady in conversation with the roast-chestnut seller; the dog asleep on the carpet in an antique shop; light on a monument; shadow in the passages.

Paris by night has a different mood altogether. On the Left Bank, when the gateman has gone home, you can wander freely among the broken statues of the Ecole Nationale Superieure des Beaux Arts feeling like an actor on the stage of a classical tragedy. Cross the Pont des Arts and enter the Louvre's still courtyards, where the magnificently-lit glass pyramid is over-looked by the old building's empty galleries with their own statues silhouetted at the windows like reclusive figures.

The greatest compliment you can pay a Parisian is to say you adore Paris – it may even engender a rare smile. Then they will offer to take you to their favourite restaurant, their small museum or little-known church and – holy of holies – share their *bonnes adresses*, the shopping secrets that ladies who lunch exchange in whispered tones at the Angelina tearooms. With this spirit in mind, we take you to discover and rediscover your own Paris.

"BUT, OH PARIS

YOUR DARK PASSAGEW

YOUR SUDDEN S

YOUR DEEP AND SILENT

WHOEVER HAS NOT HEA

BETWEEN MIDNIGHT AND

STILL KNOWS NOTHING

NOR OF YOUR STRANG

WHOEVER HAS NOT ADMIRED

AYS,

FTS OF LIGHT,

IMPASSES;

) YOUR MURMURS

TWO IN THE MORNING

OF YOUR TRUE POETRY,

E AND HUGE CONTRASTS."

HONORÉ DE BALZAC, *FERRAGUS*, 1833

ARCHITECTUR

"The form of a city changes faster than the heart of

Paris may appear static, its all too symmetrical monuments
and its thickly drawn boulevards the finished work of a vast
architect whom one can imagine sitting back, arms folded,
admiring the perfect city he has created. But in fact movement
and transition have characterized the city from its earliest days.
What gives the impression of perfection is the aesthetic sense
with which each new era added to what was already there.

Like a celebrated courtesan, Paris has been showered with
jewels from a string of illustrious lovers – kings, emperors,
presidents too, all competing for her affection. Even the Louvre
was the product of more than one dynasty. A fortress begun in
the 12th century by Philippe-Auguste, it was glorified by the
14th-century Charles V, demolished and rebuilt by François I and
his progeny, continued by Napoléons I and III, and finally given
the icing on the cake by François Mitterrand. I.M. Pei's Louvre

Pyramid sits at the very centre of an important axis, a kind of Paris ley-line, which has exerted a major pull over rulers down the centuries. Driving in from the west you approach through the futuristic La Défense with its modernist arch, up the avenue Charles de Gaulle to Napoléon's Arc de Triomphe and down the Champs-Élysées to the place de la Concorde with its obelisk, the Tuileries gardens and the Louvre. The axis continues, only slightly off-centre, with the rue de Rivoli all the way to the Bastille with its July monument now celebrating Liberty, and Carlos Ott's opera house. From the top of the Grande Arche de la Défense, on a clear day, you have a fantastic view of the axis and its layer upon layer of triumphant building.

E a mortal." Baudelaire, *Les Fleurs du Mal.*

The overview is one thing; however, the detail quite another. Despite the hazards this sometimes entails, it is rewarding to walk around Paris looking upwards. So much beauty and so many stories are written into its fabric – a lion's head here, caryatids there, an architect's signature, a tradesman's pictorial sign on a wrought-iron balcony. Viewed this way Paris is a city not of the master architect's giant hand but of human beings. Who were these people who carved angels and goddesses in stone, and whom were they thinking of as they worked?

Paris is also a city of regeneration. Municipal laws insist that façades are cleaned every decade, and life inside the buildings continues to adapt and change. What was once a bourgeois merchant's home may now be apartments, a museum or an advertising company's hi-tech offices. Boutiques displaying gorgeous creations in the window take over from dusty workshops; once-fashionable areas become seedy and poorer quarters trendy. New building continues apace, often taking something from the old as its foundations. Thus Jean Nouvel's Fondation Cartier has brought art back to Montparnasse, the former Bercy wine warehouses now spawn bars and restaurants, and the wasteland of the 13th arrondissement around the Bibliothèque François Mitterrand is in the process of becoming a new Left Bank university, where students and small industry mingle. Scratch the surface and discover a Paris living, breathing, working and changing beneath its museum-like exterior.

Looming monumentally, "solidly of the earth and yet soaringly not" as the American travel writer Donald W. George puts it, the Cathedral of Notre-Dame is the medieval heart of Paris.

CHURCHES

It is not a friendly sight, more a terrifyingly foreboding one, on the one hand because of the sheer numbers of people crowding inside it at any time of year, on the other because the edifice still comands the deep fear of the unknown that was the motivating force behind its construction. Once past the beggars (themselves like a fall-back to the Middle Ages) and milling crowds taking snaps, you are assailed by a different awareness of humanity's mass, that of the thousands of craftsmen it took to build the edifice between 1163 and 1345 – two centuries of chipping, quarrying, mortaring, buttressing and the delicate carving of its lace-like window tracery and the numerous madonnas, patriarchs, kings, saints and gargoyles. The cathedral's darkness accentuates the glory of its three rose windows, which were painstakingly removed during World War II and replaced by sandbags. Such care was not lavished on the building in previous centuries, however. By the mid-1800s, having been turned first into a Temple of Reason and then into a wine warehouse, the cathedral had fallen into such appalling disrepair that Victor Hugo wrote in 1831, "On the face of this ancient queen of our cathedrals, beside each wrinkle one inevitably finds a scar." Hugo's Notre-Dame de Paris harnessed the Romantic spirit of the day and it is largely thanks to the writing of his novel that we can enjoy the Gothic masterpiece as it is today.

Cross the place de Notre-Dame at night and it takes on the character of an Italian piazza. Brooding, silent, the cathedral holds its dark secrets while mysterious figures criss-cross in front of it – are they priests, or simply tourists in their long winter coats?

Everything else stands in the cathedral's shadow, but Paris' other churches each hold their own appeal. Saint-Chapelle is a miracle more marvellous than those it was built to house – the supposed relics brought back from Constantinople by the later canonized King Louis IX. A jewel box illumined by shafts of light casting red, yellow, blue patterns, the tiny private chapel makes the observer standing within feel as though they have walked, miniaturized, inside a kaleidoscope. The relics, recently exhibited at the Louvre, are needless to say ridiculous to the modern mind, but if they could inspire such wonder, who can castigate them?

St-Germain-des-Prés and St-Germain l'Auxerrois were both built before Notre-Dame in the clerical centre of the Left Bank, where the density of churches gives some idea of the area's importance at that time. St-Séverin is a treat for those who enjoy the flamboyant Gothic, while tiny, rustic St-Julien-le-Pauvre has a simple charm. What a pleasing dichotomy it must have seemed to the intellectuals of St-Germain, to be debating existentialism on the very café terraces opposite these temples to indefatigable faith!

More grandiose schemes decked out with marble and porphyry are to be found in the Dome of the Invalides, the wide and light basilica of St-Étienne du Mont, the colonnaded St-Sulpice and the Madeleine, that great neoclassical temple commanded by Napoléon from Poland, and now a favourite venue for society weddings.

Loathed by Parisians, loved by foreigners is Sacré-Coeur, mystical on top of the Butte Montmartre. There is something almost Disneylandesque in its phoneyness, a fairytale castle presiding over the fairground clutter below, and seedy, villagey Pigalle. For a fantasy of a completely different kind venture out to the 16th arrondissement cathedral of Alexander Nevsky, a piece of Moscow transported to bourgeois Paris, surrounded by its little Russia of restaurants and shops selling *matrioshka* dolls.

But for those in the know there is a far better – and more relaxing – way to appreciate Paris' churches. Every Sunday at 5pm, and some evenings too, churches large and small ring to the sound of music, from piano and organ recitals to gospel concerts, many of them free of charge. There are surprises in store too: a concert might tempt you into a lesser known gem such as the Syrian Orthodox church St-Ephrem-le-Syriaque, a tiny box of a church hidden in the 5th arrondissement, where a youthful string quartet performs the works of Albinoni and Mozart. Forget the guidebook for an hour or so and simply let the music fill every pore, perfectly enhancing its celestial surroundings.

The little-known church of St-Eugène in the 9th arrondissement is one of the very few that still celebrates mass in Latin. At 11am on Sundays and 7pm on weekdays, priests process with great ceremony and wafts of incense beneath the flamboyant *lustres* and brightly-painted balconies of Paris' first church constructed in iron.

Before the stern grandeur of Baron Haussmann transformed Paris there was a lighter, more aristocratic elegance – that of the 17th and 18th centuries. Majestic squares and delightful townhouses, the *hôtels particuliers*, recall this age of social grace and courtly residence, and the spirit of this era is found in the Marais, the formerly marshy land north of the Seine. Building began here in the reign of Henri IV, the pragmatic Protestant king who considered that "Paris is worth a mass", and turned Catholic forthwith.

MARAIS MANSIONS

When Henri brought stability to the city after years of religious wars he put the stamp of his absolutism on the map with the place Royale, now place des Vosges, in the Marais. Now shaded with chestnuts that would have horrified the classicists of the day, it is like an aristocratic toy-town in which Henri's favourite nobles (both Protestant and Catholic) lived side-by-side in the red-brick mansard-roofed pavilions, strolling beneath its Italianate loggias. Well-dressed children now play in the sandpit where once were staged elaborate equestrian ballets, fireworks and parades for visiting ambassadors, all of whom entered the city through this theatrical square. It was also the scene of duels in which aristocratic hotbloods fenced to the death as ladies watched from their balconies. In summer the loggias are now cluttered with restaurant tables, questionable art and busking musicians, but step through the glass doors into 28, Pavillon de la Reine, a charming and romantic hotel, and you find yourself, as if by magic, in a garden fit for Henri's queen, Marie de' Medici.

Many of the *hôtels particuliers* in the Marais have been restored and turned into museums or archives. The Hôtel Salé (literally "salty mansion", as it was named after the wealthy salt tax collector who built it in 1656) on rue de Thorigny now houses the Musée National Picasso. The spectacular courtyard is adorned by sphynxes, while its 17th-century interior, devoid of the tapestries and furniture that would originally have adorned it and opened up so that visitors can glance from room to room, provides a wonderful juxtaposition with the 20th-century artist's sculpture and paintings. Nearby, the Hôtel de Sully houses the Patrimoine Photographique, a centre for photographic exhibitions devoted to key figures or thematic shows, and the Caisse Nationale des Monuments Historiques, an archive on Paris' national monuments. The beautifully restored rooms of the *hôtel* itself are not open to the public, but just to step inside the stunning courtyard with its bas-reliefs of the elements and the seasons is to experience Louis XIII style at its most ebullient.

The Hôtel Carnavalet, once the residence of the prolific letter-writer Madame de Sévigny, is home to the Musée Carnavalet. This fabulous repository of Paris life, opened in 1880, contains interiors rescued from demolition from the Haussmann era including the 18th-century panelled Salon Ledoux from the Café Militaire in the rue St-Honoré. The museum retains much that recalls the aristocratic life of the *hôtel particuliers* in the reign of Louis XIV: its beautiful *cour d'honneur* and formal garden, and, in the panelled first-floor gallery, the Chinese lacquered desk where Mme de Sévigny wrote. The adjoining 17th-century Hôtel Le Peletier de St-Fargeau with its elegant grand staircase, is also now part of the museum, and the *orangerie* – the only surviving 17th-century one in Paris – has recently been restored.

The finest rococo interiors in Paris are to be found in the Hôtel Soubise, which houses changing historical exhibitions. It was built during Louis XIV's reign for the Prince de Soubise and his wife, Anne Chabot de Rohan, who was also a mistress of the king. The arrangement seems to have been to everyone's satisfaction and the couple rejoiced in separate apartments, both splendidly decorated by Germain Boffrand. The prince's salon has exquisite reliefs by Lemoine, while winged cherubs wielding cupid's arrow cavort in the princess's rooms.

The Marais' sparkling era lasted no more than a century, after which the mansions were transformed into workshops and tenements. It also became home to Paris' oldest Jewish community, which is remembered in the Musée d'art et d'histoire de Judaïsme in the Hôtel St-Aignan. With the restoration of so many buildings, the area is in vogue again and is now a wonderful *mêlée* of gay bars, restaurants, fashion and interiors boutiques. But on Friday nights and Saturday mornings you can still turn the corner on a deserted street and feel the full weight of history emanating from its high walls and mysterious doors.

The Medusa heads at 47 rue des Francs-Bourgeois hint at the former skullduggery within. During the American War of Independence, Beaumarchais, the librettist for Mozart's *Marriage of Figaro*, ran a fictional business as a cover for the export of arms in the fight against the English.

With its Jewish past, the Marais remains one of the best places in Paris to find sticky pastries. Oblivious to the designer shops that are now its neighbours, Finkelsztajn, on the corner of rue des Rosiers, is as homely as ever, filled with irresistible poppy seed, cream-cheese and apple delights.

Few images spell out "Paris" more clearly than its boulevards – rain-soaked, filled with the hurrying figures of a late 19th-century painting, or choked with the horse-drawn carriages and omnibuses of an early photograph. Light spills out onto the pavement from the shopfronts, broken up by the shadow of the peculiarly Parisian dome-shaped kiosks. These boulevards, built by Baron Haussmann, were a theatre where the bourgeois society of the Third Empire could promenade its new wealth while foreigners flocked to Paris to soak up the atmosphere of the age of elegance.

REVOLUTION AND REBIRTH

The 19th century was perhaps the most extraordinary era of Paris' history, when the entire fabric of the city was changed. With the accession of Napoléon III, stability was finally restored after the 1848 revolution; and to engrave this message in stone the emperor planned the creation of an imperial city, a new Rome. In the 1850s Paris was a vast building site, the likes of which had never been seen before nor has been since. Huge areas were razed, stone was torn from the ground and the serried ranks of straight façades and balconies rose up. In Baron Haussmann's rhetoric, this was war. He referred to his staff as "militant personnel" whose mission was to "go forth to the conquest of Old Paris ... ripping the quarters of the city centre from the tangle of streets virtually impenetrable to traffic" and gutting "the sordid, filthy, crowded houses which were, for the most part, but entrances to misery and disease". In today's money, the cost of this rebuild was £55,000 million.

Living in a Haussmann building still holds cachet, but these days it is the top floors that are most sought after. No longer chambres de bonnes, maids' rooms with shared bathrooms on the stairway, some have been converted into airy lofts with wide balconies and even an outdoor hot tub.

A wonderful evocation of the world of the Second Empire bourgeoisie that moved into the smart, new Paris is found at the Musée Jacquemart-André on the boulevard Haussmann itself. "Such sumptuousness should only be permitted to potentates and bankers", one journalist generously remarked after being invited to a *soirée* in Nélie Jacquemart and Edouard André's winter garden. The couple had more money to spend on art than the Louvre itself, and held sparkling musical entertainments in their mansion. However, the house they left to the nation is more than a repository of Grand Tourism gone wild. Nélie and Edouard are an endearing couple: she was a portrait painter from the wrong side of the tracks who entranced a confirmed bachelor with her love of art. Together they collected a private museum of Italian art that is better appreciated in this intimate setting then in a huge gallery. Even more touching are their private apartments – despite this being a marriage of convenience the couple decided to move their separate bedrooms nearer together; clearly, a deep affection had developed between them.

By the 1850s iron had emerged as the supreme building material. During the construction of the Gare de Lyon, Haussmann had exclaimed, "Iron, only iron". From this decade on the warlike metal became a weapon in the constantly vacillating struggle between social unrest and the onward march of the modern city. But building railway stations and department stores was one thing; building a structure that was nothing but a structure was quite another. When the Eiffel Tower went up as the triumph of the 1889 exhibition, exactly a century after the French Revolution, there were people who wondered quite what civilisation was coming to...

Seeking out Eiffel's lesser-known projects provides an interesting Paris treasure hunt. Among them are a fashionable bar in the 11th arrondissement, artists' studios in the 15th and a famous department store.

"DARN IT ALL. BUT WHAT DOES IT DO, AN EIFFEL TOWER?"
GYP, NOVELIST, 1849-1932

Indeed, apart from supporting a television aerial – a rather poor attempt at giving it a practical purpose – the tower still begs the question. This has not stopped it becoming one of the most visited monuments in the world and an icon of Paris that is instantly recognisable to people who have never even set foot on the same continent. If a city's favourite monuments in some way reflect its character there is something of the folly of Paris in the tower. Undoubtedly an engineering triumph of its day, it is also rather feminine, rather flirtatious with its lacy ironwork and bell-bottomed silhouette. If you take the trouble to go up it (tip: if you book a table in the restaurant you can jump the queue!), you will also notice an uncharacteristic bonhomie among the lift attendants and other staff who work there. What does it do, an Eiffel Tower? It lightens the heart.

Jan Morris, one of Paris' detractors, pinpoints its modernity as a defining, though sinister, quality: "There is something about the ambience, or perhaps merely the design of Paris, that makes futurism seem easily at home. Place de la Concorde, especially after dark with its lights and streaming cars, seems to me very like a space launchpad, preparing to send its obelisk into orbit." For her, the essence of Paris is La Défense, out on its futuristic limb – alienating, uncompromising, modern, but where the city's commercial heart beats.

MODERN PARIS

It is extraordinary that while other cities have their financial centres buried deep within, Paris has hers on an artery, although La Défense is joined to the city by a strong, straight line (symbolically very important in Paris), and linked by the form of its arch. Driving out at night, when the Élysées pulses with the party crowd and cars crowd bumper-to-bumper at the lights, the sight of the Grande Arche de la Défense is like a red beacon crying "modernity". Inside, the spectral city is impressive too, especially when contrasted with incongruous human activity and warmth such as the lights of a Christmas market on the plaza, where you can drink mulled wine or skate on the winter ice rink.

Paris has never shied away from modernity; if anyone, it is only its visitors who want it to remain enshrined in the rosy glow of the past. While the 20th century began with the decorated extravagance of the *beaux arts* period – the Gare d'Orsay, followed by Hector Guimard's Castel Béranger and his Métro station entrances – the shoots of modernism could be seen as early as the 1910s in the work of Henri Sauvage, especially his tiled apartment building at 6 rue Vavin. Art deco began in Paris with the Exposition des Arts Décoratifs in 1925, and was soon exported to New York; but while in Manhattan it resulted in towers of babel such as the Empire State and the Chrysler Building, in Paris deco remained, well, decorative. Typical were its public buildings, like the Palais de Chaillot, with its golden goddesses, and the rather romantic Palais de Tokyo, housing the Musée des Art Décoratifs with its dancing figures. But art deco is best appreciated on a small and cosy scale, over a coffee in Le Dôme, combined with exquisite cuisine in the restaurant Lucas Carton or the lovely mosaic-tiled Prunier.

For fans of modernism no European city is as rewarding as Paris. Here some of the great prototypes of the movement can be seen: Le Corbusier's Villa La Roche and Villa Savoy, which houses the Fondation Le Corbusier, together with his Swiss and Brazilian pavilions at the Cité Universitaire; Adolf Loos' house for Dadaist poet Tristan Tzara in the avenue Junot; and Chareau's Maison de Verre, which can normally be visited on the Journée du Patrimoine in September.

Today, Paris' architectural darlings are undoubtedly Jean Nouvel and Christian de Portzamparc. Nouvel's aesthetic echoes the glass and metal obsession of the 19th century, but in a high-tech modern style. At his Fondation Cartier de l'Art Contemporain in Montparnasse, trees rustle between transparent glass plates and one can see right into the gallery space – and even through to the lawn on the other side – from the boulevard Raspail. He created the beautiful Insitut du Monde Arabe with its myriad windows that open and close like irises, the distressed-chic interior of the Musée de la Publicité, and he has been commissioned to work his magic on the hated university campus at Jussieu. Geometric post-modernist Portzamparc is the creator of the impressive Cité de la Musique at La Villette and hip Café Beaubourg. He is now the masterplanner of the ZAC Rive Gauche project, which will rejuvenate the area around the Bibliothèque Nationale de François Mitterrand with a new Left Bank university where residential communities, small industry and education go hand-in-hand.

But the building that perhaps most represents Paris' ability to embrace the new is the Centre Pompidou. Commissioned as long ago as 1968 and completed in 1977, it was a hit from day one, both for its inside-out "boilerhouse" architecture by Rogers and Piano, and for its revolutionary content. So much had it been taken to heart by Parisians that its reopening, after repairs to damage caused by unprecedented visitor numbers, became the centrepiece of Paris' Millennium celebrations.

Paris is increasingly becoming a showcase of modern European interior design. Key addresses are the Italian group Cappellini's light-filled showcase in a former Marais *hammam*, where you can find designs by Ronan and Erwan Bouroullec, Tom Dixon, Jasper Morrison and Christophe Pillet; the Kartell Flagship Shop in the 7th arrondissement, with Ron Arad and Philippe Starck; and Sentou, designed by man of the moment, Christian Biecher, and featuring '50s classics by the likes of Arad and Eames as well as work by young designers.

If there is one thing that characterizes Paris living, it is its humanity. In every arrondissement, even those heavy with Haussmannian edifices, there is a boulangerie on virtually every

LIVING AND WORKING IN PARIS

corner – heaven forbid that anyone would think of serving up breakfast-time bread in the evening. And here, everybody walks. The city is small-scale, taxis are few, and strolling is one of the great pleasures of Paris.

Even the gendarmes have taken to rollerblading in an effort to overcome traffic gridlock. From a café table on the rue du Faubourg St-Honoré you can watch them glide by with considerable style in their *blousons*, hands clasped behind their backs like figure skaters.

Apartments are the mainstay of Paris life, be they as large as a house or the studios inhabited by students and young singles. Late 19th-century buildings were built as floors of apartments, representing a cross-section of Parisian society. The concierge's quarters were on the ground floor, the finest residences reserved for nobles and bankers on the high-ceilinged first floor, middle-class professionals and shop-keepers on the second and third, and servants and the working class on the top floor. With the advent of the lift, of course, now anything goes...

Except, perhaps, the concierge: she's becoming an endangered species, but she is still the figure that Parisians love to hate. Gossipy, grouchy, wrinkled-stockinged – everyone has a concierge story to tell. "If someone becomes really detailed, spiteful and petty in his gossip, he's likely to be upbraided with the rhetorical question, 'What are you, a concierge?'" says the writer Edmund White, who nevertheless has fond memories of Mme Denise, the euphemistic concierge of his apartment on the Île St-Louis.

Small-scale living has been tailored to a fine art. For young Parisians spring and autumn provoke the seasonal exodus to their parents to exchange winter and summer wardrobes. This provides a useful excuse for mothers to see their absent children; so everybody's happy with the arrangement. Household stores like Darty and BHV sell a mind-boggling array of tiny appliances for studio flats – ovens that fit on a shelf, vacuum cleaners that stow away invisibly and impossibly small kettles and irons. Meanwhile the fold-away Murphy-bed, the convertible sofabed and futon have whole streets of stores devoted to them. All this is part of a culture where living alone is a rite of passage. Maybe it is nostalgia for the age of the existentialists, but this is a city that celebrates individualism, where living alone, eating alone and going to the cinema alone is an assertion of freedom.

Grand Parisian living still exists too. There are apartments in the 16th arrondissement and on the Île de la Cité where 1960s panelling has been pulled down to reveal exquisite *boiserie* and Louis XIV fireplaces. Decorators such as Pierre Frey cater to classical tastes with beautiful *directoire* silks, while makers of *passementerie* (tassels and trimmings) and upholsterers have no shortage of customers. However, a new generation aspires more to New York style "loft" living. Of course, Paris doesn't really have lofts (though everyone has a cellar, even the tiniest flats). Instead, old ateliers and industrial buildings are being converted into stylish contemporary living spaces.

Offices take every shape and form, from hi-tech in at La Défense to small-scale businesses in converted ateliers. And behind Paris façades there are some surprises. Advertising firm Ogilvy Interactive occupies the fifth floor of a building on the Champs-Élysées that from the street looks like any other office complex. Inside, the pale green *boiserie* and red carpets of what was once a jewellery shop still remain, and copywriters work at their terminals under glittering Third Empire chandeliers.

Miniaturization is seen on the streets as well, from tiny dogs to nippy little Smart Cars, which are meant to be a solution to the eternal parking problem. The traditional method is to bump your way into the tiniest space – it sends Americans crazy with rage but Parisians simply shrug their shoulders. Getting around the city by any other method other is smooth and rapid. If the Métro represents in some way the soul of a city, that of Paris, coursing silently underground, only to emerge without warning to a sunlit view of Sacré Coeur or the bright expanse of the Seine, contains its element of surprise. The white- and orange-tiled stations and the pull-up door-handles are uniquely Paris; but the Métro also has a human side, animated by its roving buskers. And just when you've been in Paris long enough to hate them, when *La Vie en Rose* is beginning to grate on your nerves, a young music student alights who really can play, and smiles break out as people reach for their change.

Dogs are the bane and the delight of Paris, making this a city of heavenly skies and infernal pavements. Successive mayors have tried everything to solve the problem, from motorcycling pooper-scoopers to fines, but in the end, "plus ça change, plus c'est la même chose".

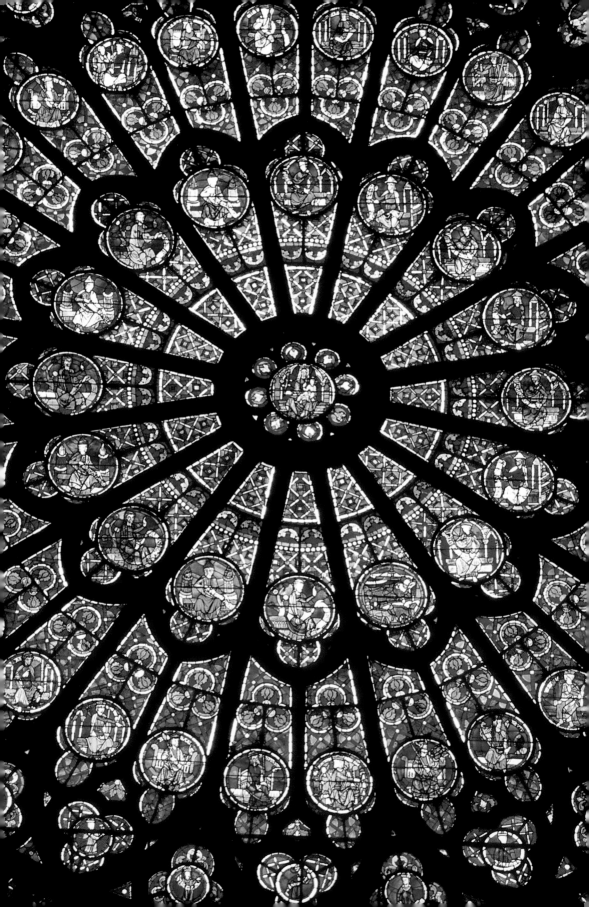

CULTURE

Where, but in Paris, do you find Racine and Rigoletto

Florence has its art, Milan has its opera, Dublin has its literature
and London has its theatre; but Paris is a fantastic melting-pot
of cultural activity. What makes it particularly exciting is the
spontaneity. While big-name concerts still sell out months in
advance, there is so much going on that you can stick a pin
in the city's listings magazines and come up with an evening of
surprising originality. If the Opéra Bastille is booked out, why
not dream to the lush sounds of a Russian Orthodox choir in
the Église St-Roch? Try out a small jazz venue, or head along
to the Maison de Radio France, whose recordings by excellent
musicians are rarely over-subscribed. What's more, the city is so
compact that you can pack two or three events into one night,
whizzing from venue to venue on the Métro with music ringing
in your ears.

As in all great cities, the most famous theatres and concert halls
are redolent with the memories of past productions and stars:

the Opéra Garnier, of course, where an ageing Maria Callas was tragically booed from the stage; the Théâtre des Champs-Élysées, where Stravinsky's *Rite of Spring* was first performed; Molière's own Comédie-Française, rehoused just after the Revolution in a beautiful building next to the Palais-Royal; and the tiny, jewel-like Opéra Comique, where *La Bohème* was premiered in France, now home to an imaginative programme of light opera and forgotten gems under its director Jérôme Savary. Classical stars have all performed at the Salle Pleyel, but far more atmospheric is the intimate Salle Cortot inside the École Normale Supérieure de Musique, or, for enchanting Chopin concerts, in summer the Orangerie in the Bois de

café-theatre and klezmer in a single night?

Boulogne. Rock and chanson legends from Frank Sinatra to Jimmy Hendrix have chalked up L'Olympia on their world tours, while more recently to pack the Zénith and the gargantuan Palais Omnisports de Paris Bercy marks the summit of a rock star's career. But discovering the smaller places is all part of Paris' allure. Chanson cafés, *péniches*, fringe theatres and multi-disciplinarian "spaces" such as the Maroquinerie or Flèche d'Or in eastern Paris offer the chance to enjoy music, dance or theatre with a more intimate, local atmosphere.

In terms of visual art and museums nowhere is more richly endowed. The city that gave birth to impressionism has guarded many of that movement's treasures in the Musée Marmottan, the Musée d'Orsay symbolically housed in the iron-built Orsay station, and the adorable Orangerie in the Tuileries gardens. There are great classical and romantic works in the constantly evolving Louvre, and modern art, magnificently displayed, in the airy heights of the Centre Pompidou and the 1930s Musée de l'Art Moderne whose new experimental offshoot in the Palais de Tokyo brings it bang up to date. But don't forget the specialized museums, the stylish Guimet with its world-class collection of Asiatic art and artefacts, the Musée de la Mode with its homage to Paris fashion, and the hundreds of smaller museums devoted to private collections, artists, writers and sometimes wonderfully absurd themes such as the fan, locks and keys, forgery, magic and even eroticism.

"The opera is a radiating centre, a sort of worldly cathedral to civilization, where art, riches, elegance hold their most splendid festivals."

Théophile Gautier, *le Moniteur universel*, 1863.

A NIGHT AT THE OPERA

Gautier's words, written when the Opéra Garnier was little more than an architect's plan, presaged the building of this opulent temple to high art and fashion. The crowning glory of the new Paris, the building was not completed until five years after the overthrow of Napoléon III, work having been inconveniently interrupted by the Prussian seige of Paris and no fewer than three Communard insurrections. When the glorious pile finally opened in 1875 it had its detractors, just like the Opéra Bastille a century on. Even Empress Eugénie, before her husband's abdication, is said to have remarked, "but it has no discernible style", to which Garnier replied, "It is the Napoléon III style", that is, marble columns, statuesque muses, golden angels trumpeting from the gables, Byzantine mosaic, red velvet and opulence of the highest degree, all of which can be seen in its brightest colours now, after the Millennium restoration.

To see the opera is one thing; to be part of a night at the opera is quite another. Many operatic performances are now held at the new Bastille site, although the Ballet National de Paris keeps the Palais Garnier as its base, but some opera productions are still held here, and are not to be missed.

Garnier, more than any other opera house in Europe, was built as a stage for its audience as much as, if not more than, the artists themselves. How could it not be, with that sweeping marble staircase lit by the gargantuan *torchères* whose light would catch the jewels around the low-cut necklines and shimmer on the emerald green, peacock and magenta of evening gowns as they swept down the steps? Imagine the scene: with the fluttering of fans reflecting the excited laughter and society gossip, the Opéra becomes a gilded cage of exquisitely exotic birds. Even the auditorium bears little relation to its ostensible purpose. Row upon row of velvet *loggias* look out at each other across the stalls, making it all the easier to wave at countess so-and-so, or flutter one's fan, conveying a message through its own secret code. On one occasion the Duke of Brunswick gave up trying to watch a performance of *The Marriage of Figaro* and played a game of chess instead. These days it may come as a surprise to find oneself sharing one of these intimate spaces, with its *chaise longue* and cosmetic mirror behind a velvet curtain, with complete strangers (the tickets are sold individually) – better perhaps to book the entire box for a romantic evening *à deux*.

The moment the conductor raises his baton, a spell is cast, and the excitement of the overture beckons you into the fantasy world of *The Magic Flute*, Puccini's Parisian tear-jerker, *La Bohéme* or one of Verdi's great tragedies. Effortlessly, the scene unfolds and from your vantage point you are drawn in, unaware of the battery of machinery and manpower flurrying behind the scenes. No other art form is as dependent on its setting for its impact, and the sense of occasion at the Opéra Garnier heightens the experience, transporting you momentarily to another age. When the interval curtain goes down sip champagne with the advertising executives and ambassadorial guests, or, even better, look down serenely from the high balconies overlooking the central hall, from which the mirror-backed champagne bar appears remarkably like Manet's *Bar at the Folies Bergères*.

One of the most magnificent sights Paris can offer is the Opéra Garnier disgorging itself at the end of a performance: hundreds upon hundreds of people stream out, down the five flights of marble stairs, past the dinner-suited programme sellers and the goddesses holding up the arch, down the wide steps at the front, and away in all directions. Within minutes the place is empty, the expanse of marble steps glistening in the aftermath of rain. A lone student walks across, clutching her books to her chest. From the warmth and bustle of l'Entracte, a café whose *raison d'être* is to feed hungry opera-goers with delicious *salades composées*, you can watch the empty scene, and on a table on the mezzanine you might perhaps recognize the soloists of the opera you have just watched, looking small and ordinary without their wigs and frock-coats, fallen angels on the world's stage.

Even in the 1950s the Opéra still had a large reservoir beneath it, in case of fire. This mysteriously became the breeding-ground of young trout (not so mysteriously really, as it was the scene shifters who had stocked it), and, in between shifts, Opéra staff used to indulge in a spot of recreational fishing.

To the hesitant visitor, or one easily swayed by the temptations of the Faubourg St-Honoré, the Louvre can take on the character of a fortress. It was, after all, used as a prison at one time in its history, and its mere enormity can be intimidating. Thankfully, while doubling the gallery space to a mind-boggling 60,000 square metres, Mitterrand's Grand Louvre project has done something to lessen this effect, with the luminous I.M. Pei Pyramid entrance flooding the underground caverns with light – while also introducing plentiful shopping opportunities for those of a material disposition. So go boldly forth: the Louvre is not nearly as monstrous as it appears.

EXPLORING THE LOUVRE

One of the fascinations of the Louvre is the way its layers of history are subsumed. The very oldest parts of the palace, Philippe-Auguste's late 12th-century fortress, were exposed during excavations for the Grand Louvre project; François I is present in the works of Leonardo, who was persuaded by the king to spend his last years in France; even Louis XVI, who preferred to live at Versailles, acquired some important Spanish and Dutch paintings and planned to open the Louvre as a museum. It was the Revolution that finally threw open the palace's doors, and thereafter Napoléon enthusiastically used the museum as a repository for the spoils of his European conquests. All the follies and conquests of the 19th century are represented here, with Louis XIII's ridiculous feather-plumed bed, Napoléon III's lavish state apartments and the porcelain collection of Adolphe Thiers, first President of the Republic.

"There is an amiably cynical rule that residents of this culture-ridden city turn up at the Pyramid in large numbers, lunch in the gourmet restaurant, take in a lecture or film, pause to inspect the glorious bookshop and go home without ever having stopped to inspect a work of art."
Helen Dudar,
The Hungry Museum.

But the secret to the Louvre is to savour just a few works or one single room. This could be the wonderful Rembrandt Gallery, where the four self-portraits show the artist at various stages in his life, the last, *Artist in his old age at his easel*, a ghostly figure peering out of the gloom; or the extraordinary Medici Gallery, where Rubens' 24 allegorical works glorified the life of Queen Marie de Medici, unabashedly resplendent with flaming hair and naked breasts. A taste for Italy might take you to the Florentine Masters; or spend an afternoon exploring the mysteries of pyramids – Egyptian rather than glass.

But beware: the Denon wing holds a dangerous concentration of great art which can have the same effect, if you are not careful, as too much chocolate. *The Winged Victory* is there, works by Fra Angelico, Botticelli, Raphael and Caravaggio, and Leonardo's mysterious and sensual *Virgin of the Rocks* (as well as the *Mona Lisa*).

First, marvel at Michelangelo's *Slaves*, designed for the tomb of Pope Julius II but given away to his friend Strozzi because they were imperfect. They found their way to the court of Henri II and later into Richelieu's collection before becoming some of the first national treasures of the Louvre during the First Republic.

Then climb the stairs to French painting, 18th century *grand oeuvres*. There is Napoléon crossing the Alps on his mule, frozen, a romantic wisp of hair crossing his face. The animal looks hang-dog, as do the two humans in the picture; but Napoléon, despite the frozen chill biting his neck and the air of defeat, fixes you with his unyielding stare. A decade earlier there is Napoléon regal on the battlefield of Eylau, and Baron Gros' strange depiction of him as a healer, visiting the plague-stricken at Jaffa; and David's wry documentary of the Emperor's self-coronation, including Napoléon's sour-faced mother looking on, despite the fact that she refused to attend the ceremony. There are many, many other great works in the Denon, but these portraits of Napoléon resonate with the history of Paris and of the building itself, revealing something of why Paris still sees Napoléon not as the man who met his Waterloo, but as the Romantic hero who demanded to be laid to rest "on the banks of the Seine, in the midst of the French people whom I have loved so dearly".

Don't give in to the temptation to see yet one more gallery, one more work of art, until urgent ushering out by the museum staff comes as a welcome relief. Time must be left to soak up the last rays of sunshine in the Tuileries, to admire the blushing pink pillars of Napoléon's mini Arc de Triomphe, to sit in the Café Marly under the arcades, named after the great horses in the museum, enjoy a *citron pressé* or a *kir* and reflect on the day's rich images.

After the Louvre, those still unsated can stroll through the Tuileries to the small Jeu de Paume gallery, whose temporary exhibitions on modern art have included Picasso Érotique and Eduardo Chillida. It's an airy antidote to the palace itself.

The French often refer to cinema as "le septième art", a phrase redolent with meaning: as well as putting film-making up there with painting, music, drama and the rest of the so-called fine arts, it adds a faint mystique, with its echoes of sixth sense and the ancient occult magic of the number seven.

THE CINEMA

The phrase also conveys some of the fascination, or obsession, that Paris has for cinema. The city of Marcel Carné, of Renoir, Truffaut and Godard adores its native talent, but also appreciates quality film-making from around the world. Where else would 2,000 people turn up in a gypsy encampment in the middle of August for a free screening of a lesser-known Fellini documentary, virtually rioting when they were turned away because only 200 could fit inside? Whole seasons are devoted to a single Japanese director; retrospectives on fringe members of the *Nouvelle Vague* are regularly held, along with seminars and interviews with directors. The love of cinema reaches out into other aspects of life too. In the Marais, the charmingly ramshackle Hôtel du Septième Art has rooms filled with torrid posters from the heyday of Hollywood, while in the rue Lemercier in the 17th arrondissement there is a barber's called L'Atelier where you can be shorn amid film canisters and a floor-to-ceiling collage of cinema stars. In a back street in the 20th arrondissement Le Casque d'Or restaurant pays loving tribute to Jacques Becker's film of the same name, starring Simone Signoret and shot in the area in the 1950s.

Paris is undergoing a renaissance as a film location, and canteens and lighting equipment are often to be seen camped outside its restaurants and cafés. But, says director and scenarist Michel Muntz, finding locations is not as easy as you might expect – jealous *coproprietaires* of shared buildings often vote against an owner inviting film-makers in.

The locations for glorying in this year-long festival of film can be as sumptuous or evocative as the films themselves. Take the Grand Rex, an art deco extravaganza that has been operating as a cinema since 1932. Designed by Auguste Bluysen, with fantasy Hispanic interiors by John Eberson, it's as likely to be showing a dubbed American blockbuster as a French film, but is a must for reliving cinema's Radio Days heyday – it also provides fascinating backstage tours. The Pagoda provides an even more exotic setting. Built at the height of the '20s craze for *Chinoiserie*, it was once almost bought by the Chinese embassy, which pulled out when it discovered that one of the decorations features a famous defeat by the Japanese.

Cinémathèques, the tiny film houses of the Left Bank, are one of the enduring features of the quarter's intellectual past. It was in these cinemas that Sartre, according to Simone de Beauvoir, used to sob into his handkerchief, adding a new dimension to the stony-faced philosopher. Arthouse cinemas such as Action Écoles, Reflet Medici Logos and Montmartre's Studio 28, a tiny cinema filled with memories which has the footprints of many famous *cinéastes* imbedded in its forecourt, are national treasures which amazingly manage to survive despite competition from multiplexes. Don't miss the chance to go to the Forum des Images in Les Halles. A remarkable national archive, containing every film ever made about Paris, it's is housed in a Kubrickesque studio where robots collect the films from the archive and you sit in black leather chairs with built-in earphones. The archive is soon to be digitized and will surely lose some of its unique atmosphere while gaining in viewing quality. It organizes original programmes of events, but is itself a cinematic paeon to the city.

Paris, uniquely, knows how to bring cinema alive. Every year the park at La Villette holds a summer of free outdoors cinema on a huge inflatable screen, to which thousands converge with picnics, rugs or deckchairs. Other annual events include Cinéma au Clair du Lune, a joint French and Italian initiative, screening films shot in Paris in the open air, close to their actual locations or to somewhere that conjures up the atmosphere of the film. A film that epitomises Paris in the late '50s, *À Bout de Souffle*, was screened on the Square Marigny, with the distant roar of traffic on the Champs-Élysées adding to the atmosphere. A serious crowd camped on the grass made up of film students and those that remembered the heady days of 1959, when the *Nouvelle Vague auteurs* first broke the rules of French cinema. And you never know, at this kind of occasion there might be an appearance by one of the many stars who still make Paris their home – Catherine Deneuve, who makes the daily pilgrimage to Poilâne for her bread, or Jean-Paul Belmondo, who is often seen tucking into the dish named after him at his favourite Italian restaurant.

All credit to the Montmartre café that features in the film *Amélie Poulain*. Far from capitalizing on its fame, the Café des Deux Moulins retains its slightly grubby, workaday atmosphere, with just a poster of the film pinned up in the corner. One almost expects to see the film's rheumy tobacconist sitting in her booth.

"Atmosphère! Atmosphère!" the actress Arletty famously exlaimed in front of the Hôtel du Nord, in Marcel Carné's film of the same name. The Canal St-Martin setting was actually reconstructed in a studio, but the real Hôtel du Nord with its tiled lobby is genuinely atmospheric and acquiring new fame as an Anglophone comedy venue.

TREASURE HOUSES OF PARIS LIFE

The French call them *musées sentimentaux*, small museums, often in the homes of painters and writers, which preserve the spirit of an age as much as the work of a particular artist. Even if your time in Paris is short, it is worth devoting an afternoon to one of the city's pocket treasures that can easily become a favourite haunt, away from the crowded boulevards and packed national museums.

Musée de la vie Romantique

A museum of Romantic life – what could be more Parisian? In fact, this house museum in the former home of Ary Scheffer devoted to Georges Sand and her circle celebrates an aristocratic-cum-bohemian crowd that was largely made up of *émigrées*. La Nouvelle Athènes, as the area was called, was a meeting point for such luminaires as Chopin, Sand, Delacroix and Charpentier. The museum itself, while showing little of the life of this circle apart from from *objets d'art* and mementos, is a charming place to while away an afternoon. The gallery often hosts interesting special exhibitions, and the tea garden is run by a man of such a romantic disposition that it takes him a good half hour merely to prepare your tray of Bailkal tea, a slice of orange cake and a complimentary saucer of parma violets.

Atelier-Musée Henri Bouchard

Bouchard, who was responsible for the monumental Apollo for the Palais de Chaillot, may not be Paris' most famous sculptor, but the studio where he moved in 1924 is evocative of the life of an artist in the first half of the 20th century. Lovingly tended by the sculptor's son and daughter-in-law, the studio has been preserved in all its dusty array – crammed with sculptures, casts, moulds, sketchbooks and tools – as if the scuptor could walk in and start work at any moment.

Musée Edith Piaf

The epitome of a *musée sentimental*, the French singer's museum, open by appointment only, is the work of devoted fans and friends of Piaf. It consists of two rooms in the area where the "little sparrow" first walked from bar to bar singing, and has touching exhibits, including her tiny dresses and shoes, letters, posters and photos.

Musée Nissim de Camondo

A private collection put together by a well-off banker, Count Moïse de Camondo, this is especially poignant as it was designated a museum in memory of the count's son Nissim, who died in World War I. Thereafter, the rest of the family was killed at Auschwitz. The collection includes French furniture and ceramics, Italian marble, carpets and tapestries. These are French national treasures; but it is of the tragedy of the Camondo family, and so many others like them, that the museum speaks so powerfully.

Musée du Crystal Baccarat

Baccarat's showroom is one of the many surprises to be found in the 10th arrondissement; and, far from the fashionable shopping crowd, this "Paradise road" is full of glassmakers' workshops. In a rather glamorous '70s showroom filled with mirrors are the technically brilliant crystal creations of the exhibitions of 1878, 1889 and 1990, together with a fascinating litany of fallen heads of state who once drank out of the celebrated designer's glasses. The most unexpected exhibits are the perfume bottles from 1851 that clearly presage art deco motifs.

Musée de L'evantail

The museum of the fan is not such an out-dated idea when you see today's Métro passengers in the heat of August fanning themselves with cheap Chinese fans bought in Belleville. The fan-making Hoguet family's collection includes exquisite 18th-century fans with mother-of-pearl handles through to Karl Lagerfeld's variations on a theme. Until the French Revolution, only the nobility were allowed to use fans; whether or not because of this, the language of fans is a minefield of misunderstanding and understatement.

Musée Gustave Moreau

This is known as the most eccentric museum in Paris. Moreau, a Symbolist artist of note but not of genius, was determined that his work should live on after his death, and so designated his home as a museum. A shy man who continued to live with his parents, he filled his posthumous apartment with canvases of John the Baptist, St George, griffins, unicorns and lascivious Salomés.

Musée Zadkine

A prime example of a museum whose value extends far beyond its treasures, the museum dedicated to the Russian artist Zadkine is a delightful garden not far from Montparnasse, containing the last vestiges of the vanished world of the Montparnasse ateliers. Ossip Zadkine lived at the address from 1928 until his death in 1967, except for those years he spent in exile from wartime anti-Semitism, when his wife, Valentine Prax, hid his sculptures in their neighbours' cellars. Zadkine's work runs the full gamut of styles, from primitivist, through elongated faces influenced by Modigliani, to cubist. Some of his poetry is also on display.

On 29 May 1913 there was a riot in Paris. There were no barricades: it took place, in fact, in a theatre just off the Champs-Élysées. The cause was the first performance of Stravinsky's *The Rite of Spring*. The perpetrators read like an all-star cast of early 20th-century culture: Diaghilev staged the production, Picasso painted the sets and Nijinsky was the soloist; but the audience behaved more like a crowd at a boxing match, whistling and booing on the one hand and shouting with glee on the other. In the red corner, Camille Saint-Saëns, who left the theatre in indignation, the Austrian ambassador, who laughed, and the Princess de Purtales, who exclaimed "this is the first time that anyone dared to make a fool of me!" In the blue corner, Ravel, repeatedly shouting "Genius!" and Debussy, pleading for quiet. One society lady spat in the face of a detractor as her escort challenged him to a duel, while backstage Stravinsky had to restrain the normally effeminate Nijinsky from going out and attacking members of the audience.

PARIS AND THE AVANT-GARDE

Paris has always courted controversy in the arts. After all, it was here that the Californian Isadora Duncan began her barefoot revolution (her grave in Père Lachaise cemetery attracts almost as many devotees as that of Jim Morrison). In art, cubism, impressionism, fauvism and surrealism all had their roots here. These days the avant-garde tradition is proudly nurtured. At 1 place Igor-Stravinsky you will find an underground bunker, an annex to the Centre Pompidou, which houses IRCAM, the foundation designed to foster experimental composition. Its output has been criticized for inaccessibility, but more recently it has borne fruit with daring and diverse offerings as part of the summer Agora festival, including dance and film music. The Cité de la Musique at La Villette, where the new Conservatoire is situated, is also hosting a wider range of musical styles, and you can see stars-to-be perform for free in student concerts.

In terms of dance Paris has probably seen more experimentation than any other city this century. Native choreographers have shocked with nudity, played with hi-tech computer effects, and are now swapping barefoot for trainers in hip-hop and street-influenced dance. Some of the best venues for contemporary dance are the Théâtre de la Bastille, with a strongly avant-garde international menu; Le Regard du Cigne, which promotes new choreographic talent in a Belleville barn; and the Théâtre de la Ville, which regularly sees famous names such as Anne Teresa de Keersmaeker and Pina Bausch. The Centre National de la Danse's Studio, CND, welcomes innovative choreographers performing short works and works-in-progress, and L'Étoile du Nord concentrates on an off-beat, multimedia contemporary dance scene. Dance fans also get the yearly treat of the highbrow Festival d'Automne in venues all around Paris, with which Merce Cunningham has been involved for 30 years.

Paris also offers a vibrant world music and dance scene. Cultural institutes such as the Insitut du Monde Arabe and the Iranian Cultural Centre host visiting artists from jazz to sufic drumming. The Centre Mandapa is an Indian dance and music centre that also invites companies from China, North Africa and Eastern Europe, while Théâtre de la Ville's second venue, the Théâtre des Abbesses, has Indian and flamenco performances. One of Paris' greatest assets, injecting huge amounts of energy not only into dance performance but also training and education, is Georges Momboye. This Ivory Coast native who trained with Alvin Ailey in New York runs the only state-funded African dance school in France: his approach to dance defies any stereotypes. Contemporary, mime, traditional village dances, hip-hop – he says all are African dance forms, and, despite his international status, he teaches at grass-roots level.

These days Paris welcomes avant-garde artists with open arms. In the galleries of Marais you can find video art by the likes of Pierrick Sorin and Steve McQueen and installations by Thomas Hirshhorn and Rikrit Tiravanija. Conceptual art is concentrated in the galleries on the rue Louise-Weiss behind the Bibliothèque de France François Mitterrand. Art Collectives are a lively feature of the Paris scene, active in shopping malls, hairdressers and, most recently, the area around the Palais de Tokyo, which has reopened as the new Site de Création Contemporaine. Here, in a '30s building shared with the Musée d'Art Moderne, is Paris' largest space for contemporary art, along with resident artists, talks, fashion shows, DJs and a café to encourage debate – this is Paris, after all.

Living in an "artists' squat" is the latest expression of *la vie bohème* in Paris. With 10 per cent of the city's property uninhabited, the authorities are actually encouraging this creative use of previously rat-infested properties. The best squats are highly organised and far from anti-commercial. Chez Robert-Electron Libre, above the high street shops on the rue de Rivoli, welcomed 40,000 art lovers in 2002 and auctions are held attracting buyers with serious money to spend.

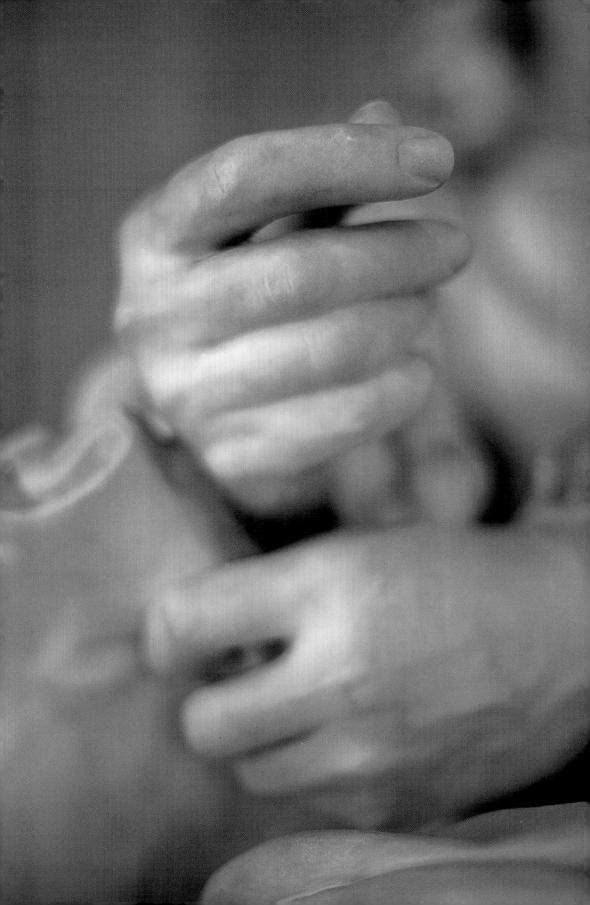

RETAIL

Even the packaging's perfect in this city of earthly

INDULGENCE

Paris without shopping is like *tarte Tatin* without the cream. To stroll down the wide pavements of the avenue Montaigne past the most famous names in Parisian fashion has a glamour that is quintessentially Paris. Dior, Chanel, Yves St Laurent, Balenciaga – all still carry the cachet that made their collections headline news in the '50s and '60s, transforming the "golden triangle" of the 8th arrondissement into their domain. Similarly, the place Vendôme and the Faubourg St-Honoré are synonymous with a luxe and style that simply will never go out of fashion.

Then there is the historical splendour of the *grands magasins*, whose flamboyant 19th-century architecture proclaims them cathedrals of commerce, and the chic shopping district of St-Germain, whose fashion names, often mirroring those found on the Right Bank, are joined by smart homeware shops selling the most exquisite linen, glass, ceramics and top-of-the-range cookware.

However, shopping in Paris has another dimension: by doing a bit more legwork, a bit more preparation and tracking down the small boutiques that are unique to the city, you can unearth wonderful finds that are in their own way more exclusive than a Louis Vuitton bag or Hermès scarf. Young designers are currently in their element, and the hottest new talents can be found in the Marais, around the Bastille and even in the passage Vivienne: the 19th-century covered passages are undergoing a revival, and beautiful shops selling rarities such as hand-made silk flowers and glassware sit side-by-side with eccentric businesses that have been there since the age of the surrealists.

delights, where shopping is an art form.

For antique and bric-à-brac hunters, Paris is a wonderland, from the specialized showrooms of the Louvre des Antiquaires, a gallery of 500 dealers near the Palais-Royal, to the auction houses and the sprawling and unpredictable *marchés aux puces*. There is also the chance to stumble upon a bargain at a *brocante*, one of the ephemeral street markets that spring up on Sundays and holidays. Here, the atmosphere is more like that of a country sale, though the same cannot be said of the prices.

Unusually for such a cosmopolitan city, Paris is still the home of countless artisans. If you look beyond the street, down passageways and under arches, in the traditional manufacturing districts, you enter a lost world of craftsmen and restorers whose skills have been passed down through the generations. This strong tradition is seen in the contemporary context of young jewellery and furniture designers working independently and selling from small shops with a workshop attached.

There is something else that makes shopping in Paris delectable, and can even turn the most hardened shopophobe into a convert – the art of presentation. Whatever you buy, from a bouquet of flowers to a pair of shoes, your purchase will be lovingly wrapped with tissue paper, ribbon and a tiny label. If you are buying a present, most shops also gift-wrap, which is done with such artistry that one wonders if there are schools to teach this finishing touch that makes the whole shopping experience just that little bit more pleasurable.

Is there something different about the way the French shop? Certainly, to shop in Paris successfully requires practice, but once mastered it becomes utterly addictive. The key can be found in the phrase *"lèche-vitrines"*. While other nations merely window-shop, the French, to translate literally, lick their shop windows. It is this zeal that gives rise to their shopping finesse.

THE GREAT AGE OF SHOPPING

Neither will they be thwarted in their mission by shop assistants. Dressed for combat, with a clear idea of what she is looking for, the French shopper will enter the chosen emporium assertively with a "Bonjour madame", pre-empting the shop assistant's interrogatory "Voulez-vous quelque chose?" by asking for something that the shop probably does not have. The negative answer, or the attempt to palm them off with something different, then provides the excuse for a condescending pout.

Shopping by flirtation demands a set of skills in which the French are trained at birth. "Alongez-vous," exhorts the theatrical owner of the futon shop on the rue du Faubourg St-Antoine. "Ah, mais vous êtes mignonne comme ça!" Have you ever bought a bed because you look good lounging on it?

All of which makes it surprising that the grand magasin, with its more impersonal mode of shopping, where you can look and flirt with the goods largely unhindered, ever took off. This major revolution in shopping arrived after the Paris Commune of 1871 with the opening of Galeries Lafayette, Printemps, La Samaritaine and Le Bon Marché. These were the first shops to carry a variety of "fancy goods" at fixed prices, and on account of their profusion of glittery merchandise were considered by some to be immoral. Gustave Macé, Chief of Security at the time, went so far as to describe them as "an abyss, a Babel, a spider web" where, "with her little bird's head the daughter of Eve enters into this inferno of coquetry like a mouse into a mousetrap". At Galeries Lafayette nowadays, men while away the time at the cigar counter or Internet café while their wives and girlfriends shop.

Today, when department stores dominate every city centre, the *grands magasins* are still magnificent. The stained-glass dome of Galeries Lafayette, La Samaritaine's elaborate turquoise and gilded ironwork and magnificent atrium, Printemps' art nouveau cupola made of 3,185 pieces of glass, and Le Bon Marché's zig-zag escalators by chic designer Andrée Putnam, all give shopping an almost operatic quality. The stores are constantly trying to outdo each other with cutting-edge departments as billboard war wages across the platforms of the Métro. Galeries Lafayette now has Le Labo, a style lab for progressive international designers such as Alexandre Matthieu, Gaspard Yurkievich, Tom Liegen and Xuly Bët, and five fashion and beauty consultants to guide you through the maze, while arch-rival Printemps , majoring on luxury goods with its new Printemps de la Mode store, also has a "literary café" and Didier Ludot vintage couture concession.

DIY department store BHV may sound like an unlikely setting for romance, but its café and DIY lectures have become a hot spot for young singles looking for a mate – at least they know whether he or she can wire up a plug.

The twenties was the age of the luxury boutique, when the avenue Montaigne and place Vendôme first became the home of names such as Chanel and Cartier. However much luxury becomes a commodity, prey to fashion and available in unintimidating form in department stores, these shops will remain the ultimate expression of that exclusivity.

A few years ago, however, a concept arrived that once again overturned ideas of how to shop. It started with Colette, the now famous lifestyle store on the rue St-Honoré, which displays minimalist trinkets under glass, has its own Japanese language magazine and CD, and a fashion floor where one wanders between headless models displaying the week's chosen designs. Paradoxically, Colette represents a return to a quaint, old-fashioned kind of shopping where style choices are made by the shop rather than the customer, and you have to ask before you touch. Seeing its success (its water bar is still the hippest lunch spot in the area), concept stores are now multiplying, from aristocratic Jean-Charles de Castelbajac's personal vision, heavily influenced by '70s futurism, to Spree in Montmartre, where owners Bruno Hadjadj and Roberta Oprandi (artist and fashion designer respectively) juxtapose art, furniture design and fashion.

Colette really does think of everything. In a rainstorm customers entering the shop are handed plastic covers for their umbrellas, to prevent them dripping on the floor.

LES BONNES ADRESSES

Trading shopping secrets – which can range from a rush-seated chair mender, to a "stock" shop (discounted end-of-line labels), to a newly discovered young designer – is a Parisian obsession. We offer our selection for the visitor to Paris intent on finding delights not known to everyone.

Fashion

Amin Kader's tiny boutique in the 6th arrondissement is a well-kept secret. The Berber couturier supplies Arran-knit cashmere pullovers, elegant raincoats, hand-stitched travel bags and beauty products from a Florentine church. A few streets away is Le Cachemirien, where Italian designer Rosenda Arcioni works directly with Kashmiri artisans creating designs that blend tradition and modernity. Exquisitely embroidered shawls come in an array of natural shades. Two native designers whom the French have been selfishly keeping to themselves are Severine Peraudin, who makes evening-wear reminiscent of *millefeuille* in superfine layers of stretch polyamide, and Paule Ka, the label created by Serge Cajfinger, whose satin, organza and taffeta pieces have a touch of Jackie O style about them.

Flowers

Christian Tortu is universally acknowledged as *the* Parisian florist, and his St-Germain shop seeks perfection in all things. But there is something about Paris that makes artistry blossom even in humble quarters. Around the Gare de Lyon there is a cluster of florists including the delightful and original Arôm. Its two owners, Saber and Fabien, have filled the tiny shop with busts, African sculptures and a jungle of woodland flowers. Their posy of anemonies wrapped in raffia and brown paper makes an enchanting dinner party offering.

Household

Cooks make a beeline for E. Déhillerin, which has served professional chefs since 1820. This no-nonsense warehouse has vast copper pots hanging from the ceiling, a huge selection of knives and all sorts of peculiar culinary gadgets. Dîners en Ville is a beautiful shop displaying both antique and new tableware that defies the minimalist trend. Especially covetable is the large collection of bone- and glass-handled cutlery. Very chic, very expensive sheets, table linen, shirts, candles and furniture come in white, cream, grey, chocolate and black at Catherine Memmi – it's all terribly Parisian. If your tastes veer more towards soft kashmiri throws, low-lying sofas or embroidered Moroccan bathrobes, put your trust in Françoise Dorget, whose eye is spot-on. Everything in her shops – Caravane and Caravane Chambre 19 – is covetable.

Jewellery

Naïla de Monbrison is a name in the diary of every jewellery aficionado in Paris. In dark wood cabinets the gallery exhibits exquisite original pieces, from silver necklaces like a breastplate to a ring made from a quail's egg. Regular exhibitors include Sylvie Vari and Georgio Vigna. At La Reine Margot, Gilles Cohen has invited international jewellers to create modern pieces using ancient stones, amulets, seals and scarabs. For antique jewellery, Lydia Courteille has a talented eye and is trusted by such famous customers as Catherine Deneuve to find them exquisite and unusual pieces – the collection in her St-Honoré shop ranges from a Tunisian engagement necklace carved with birds, to an Empire tiara, while her Rive Gauche shop specializes in 20th-century designers such as Suzanne Belpesson and René Boivin. While you are on the Left Bank don't miss Irina Volkonski, a young Russian in Paris who designs costume jewellery with a surreal flair using such materials as wood from the great gale and resin.

Lingerie

Paris invented it, and Paris takes it very, very seriously – visit the svelte shop at Erès in the smart 8th arrondissement for demure, beautifully cut lingerie and swimwear. Exquisite, made-to-measure creations are found at Alice Cadolle, whose daughter Poupie is the fifth generation of her family to work in the business. The Belle Époque studio is open by appointment for fittings but there is also a ready-to-wear range of bodices and corsets that have become an intrinsic part of Christian Lacroix and Thierry Mugler's collections.

Musical Instruments

It is astonishing how many musical instrument makers and repairers are found in Paris' backstreet passages. The most wonderful is Orphée, more of a museum than a shop. Peer through the window into the dark recesses and you'll see what

amounts to a mythological bestiary of instruments, from serpent-like reed instruments to dulcimer and aeolian harps. C.S. Lewis would have adored it.

20th Century Collectables

If you want to take a little bit of the Belle Époque home with you visit À l'Imagerie, which stocks a host of original posters from circus and cabaret, cigarette advertising, 1920s travel posters and old fashion plates. For '50s-'70s kitsch without trawling through the flea markets, Fiesta Gallerie is a Marilyn-era treasure trove with juke boxes, enormous '60s lamps and bizarre wig stands.

Scent

Perfumes are no longer the preserve of the couture houses. If nostalgia is your thing, visit Parfums Caron, whose noses have managed to recreate the house's classic scents from 1914-54 – a potentially Proustian experience. In the little art deco boutique on the avenue Montaigne, the scents are displayed in glass phials like samovars. In contrast, Éditions de Parfums Frédéric Malle is housed in a swish showcase designed by Olivier Lempereur and Andrée Putnam. Here eight exclusive perfumes are made by top creators commissioned by the former consultant for Lacroix and Hermès.

Stationery

What a joy, in the age of the computer, to find hand-made paper. Calligrane's three shops have every shade and texture of paper including some encrusted with petals, and the Comptoir des Écritures specializes in calligraphy with inks, pens, hand-made paper as well as courses and exhibitions.

At the end of the 18th century visiting your tailor or ordering a hat could be a hazardous business. Then speculators had the bright idea of creating covered passageways, arcades lined with bright shopfronts where the shopper for the first time could browse the goods on offer, take tea in the various salons, promenade and mingle. *Flânerie* (browsing) became fashionable. The stage was set for Paris to become the shopping capital of the world.

COVERED PASSAGEWAYS

Between 1791 and 1860 more than 150 *passages couverts* were built. Few remain. They were put out of business by the *grands magasins*, became the haunts of prostitutes and pimps, and many were destroyed in the course of new building. Those that survive are some of the true delights of Paris. In the past 15 years they have seen a revival: new shops have opened, old ones been revitalised and tea-rooms and restaurants are again thriving. But, just as if the ghosts of the passages, so beloved by the surrealists, have kept watch over them all these years, a mysterious quality lingers on; they are the magic toyshops of the heart.

This spirit is strongest in the passages off the *grands boulevards*, especially Passage des Panoramas and passage Jouffroy, which embrace the two ends of the era. Today, Passage des Panoramas looks Christmassy all year round, with its arches of lights decked with trailing ivy. Here, among the philatelists' and trinket shops, you'll find two businesses that evoke the age when visiting cards were really used for visiting. Mercier, Graveur Imprimeur, at number 8, still has an ancient printing press that is used on occasion. When can you see it in action? "Ça dépend," replies the charming girl running the shop. The printer spends most of his time now in the suburb of Lavallois, but you might be lucky. You can also buy all the paraphernalia to revive the art of writing – quill pens, inkpots, paper. A little further down on the opposite side is Stern, whose dusty shop-window contains menus, vignettes, ex libris and heraldic plates which can be reprinted in batches of ten. Nearby is a modern atelier using the ancient technique of marquetry to create beautiful deco-inspired furniture. On Sundays, when the shop is closed, you can see the two craftsmen, Kamel Ennebati and Cesario Noré, working together at their art with an enviable absorption. You can eat pizza in a recreation of an English railway carriage or enjoy nursery food (fluffy *oeufs en cocotte* or even boiled eggs) and cakes at *salon de thé* l'Arbre à Cannelle.

Cross the boulevard Montmartre and you are in the passage Jouffroy – not built until 1847. It feels the most theatrical of the passages, perhaps because of the Grévin waxworks museum and the exotic emporium stocking costumes and sitars from Rajasthan; perhaps also because the ghosts of the Petit Casino café-concert, the marionnettes and the Séraphim Chinese shadow puppet theatre still linger imperceptibly. At number 34 is the celebrated M.G.W Segas' cane gallery. M. Segas himself is as flamboyant as the antique canes he sells, dressed in a green shirt and leather waistcoat with a handsome handlebar moustache, though he claims not to be dandy enough to go out carrying a cane. His shop, lit by chandeliers that grow out of the floor like trees, contains part of his 1,500-strong collection of canes, featuring greyhounds, Mandarins' heads, reclining nudes and just about anything else you can think of on their handles. There is also a wonderful toyshop, Pain d'épices, and at the end the cosy Hôtel Chopin, named after the composer who lived nearby.

At the other end of the spectrum is the elegant galerie Vivienne, whose fashion history is being revisited in the form of the young designers who have set up shop, including Nathalie Garçon. Open the creaky door of Jousseaume's antiquarian bookshop, and you can breathe deeply the evocative smell of old books and chat to the owner, who appears blinking like a mole from the depths of his office. There is Emilio Robba, whose artificial flowers are so real that it is only the absence of perfume that will convince you of the illusion, and, at the entrance to the *galerie*, Legrand Filles et Fils, a very pukka wine shop. Francine Legrand, the charming third generation owner, explains how the business followed the fortune of the *galerie*, being whittled down to a warehouse and *épicerie*, but now once again thriving with a stylish shop specializing in wine accessories from corkscrews, tasting glasses and decanters to books.

Passage des Panoramas is named after the two rotondes where the American James Thayer presented his "panoramas", a crowd-puller whose appeal is hard to understand today. Approaching through dark corridors, you entered the dome and were surrounded by painted canvases on all sides depicting a real scene, with the perspective so exactly done that it gave a sense of "another reality". Historical scenes were popular, such as "the Evacuation of Toulon by the English in 1793".

While Americans go to Harry's Bar or Haynes, passage Brady has become the haunt of homesick Britons pining for the taste of curry – it is lined with Indian restaurants. At the Indian grocers at the end, among the bindis and incense, you can also buy Marmite and Bird's Eye custard!

"Who would have thought that Europe contained so much old junk? Or that, the servant class having disappeared, hearts nostalgic for the bourgeois epoch would hunt so eagerly for Empire breakfronts, Récamier sofas and curule chairs?"
Saul Bellow, *Old Paris*, Granta 10, 1984.

BROCANTES AND THE PUCES

Who indeed? It sometimes seems as if Paris is one enormous fleamarket. Like a vast maturing cheese, the acres of junk that emerge from the Portes de Vanves, Montreuil and Clignancourt spread their veins through underpasses and carparks in an attempt to permeate the city. Meanwhile, their spores travel in, popping up at weekend *brocantes*, *dépot ventes* (second-hand furniture shops) and *vide-greniers* – literally "empty attics".

Paris fleamarkets run the gamut, from piles of old batteries and mismatched nuts and bolts, broken watches and jumpers that have been washed cardboard stiff at Montreuil to fine art deco and '50s furniture at Clignancourt. Don't expect much of a bargain, but the sheer scale of the *puces* makes them fascinating to wander around – they are a great repository of social history.

Paris' fleamarket tradition stems from the *chiffoniers* (a most poetic name for rag-and-bone-men) and *ferrailleurs* (scrap metal merchants), who, being social rejects, were kept outside the city boundaries. Nowadays many of the traders are experts in their field. In the coolly collectable field of '50s-'70s design, for instance, Marine Garnier runs Ludlow, a showroom within the Marché Malassis at Clignancourt that appears to come straight out of the pages of a modern interiors magazine. Original furniture by the likes of the Eames, Kagan and Robsjohn Gibbings is carefully picked for its design credentials and impeccable condition. Books and catalogues illustrate the furniture and its prototypes. "There are four specialist dealers in this era at Clignancourt, and a showroom at Montreuil with six antiquaries," she says. "It's very collectable at the moment, and this is the very top end of the market."

In total contrast, the market at Vanves in the south of the city is the smallest and friendliest, full of colourful stands where collectors of small, sparkly and sentimental items are in heaven

– costume jewellery, dolls, old photographs, crystal, eau de Cologne bottles, Belle Époque biscuit tins, lace and buttons offer the opportunity to cart back enough ephemera to recreate Colette's apartment in your own home.

Montreuil is the most souk-like of the *puces*, disgorging mountains of debris from the cellars of Paris apartment blocks. The market traders yell out their wares and fat ladies push you out of the way in their efforts to get at the fake CK underwear, but with a true bargain-hunter's tenacity you may find a trophy among the new and the way past its sell-by date.

Brocantes (travelling flea markets) spring up at well-known junctions, often on Sundays and bank-holidays. You must look for the banners strung across the roads advertising them about a week in advance. Most of these attract professional dealers selling art and artefacts, but they are an interesting hunting-ground, the urge to buy (even at not very bargain prices) compounded by their ephemeral nature. *Vide-greniers*, on the other hand, are more of a fun occasion for people to nose around in what their neighbours had been storing up in their attics. People are shameless in what they will display – appalling taste in records, clothes, unwanted wedding presents – but the prices suggest they are loathe to part with these things after all!

Perhaps the biggest cabinet of curiosities, however, is Drouot, the umbrella organization for Paris' independent auctioneers. Prestige sales now take place in the avenue Montaigne salerooms, but a visit to the less glamorous 9th arrondissement Hôtel Drouot makes for a highly entertaining afternoon. Advance information on sales is published in the weekly Gazette de l'Hôtel Drouot and, once inside the building, which has the air of a '70s airport lounge, visitors can wander freely among the various previews, travelling from floor to floor by escalator. Here you might find Belle Époque posters in one room, silverware in another and a bizarre collection of ecclesiastical objects in another, while the auctioneers, aided by black-mandarin-jacketed assistants, sell Oriental carpets or lesser-known works by '30s painters. Surprisingly enough, Drouot is one of the most accessible auction houses in the world, and it could just be the source of the best bargains in Paris.

For carefully selected – but highly priced – antiques, browse in the Louvre des Antiquares on place du Palais Royal. In a rarified atmosphere behind the façade of a former *grand magasin* you'll find 250 dealers specializing in anything from Russian jewellery to nautical antiques.

Drouot can no longer rest on its laurels. Antiquated laws have finally been changed to allow Christie's and Sotheby's to hold sales in Paris. These two houses are attracting famous names, including the collections of Charles-Otto Zieseniss and Karl Lagerfeld.

A world away from the *grand magasins* and the boutiques of St-Germain, there are still artisans employing traditional skills in a time scheme from another age. Ten minutes walk from Bastille, you would hardly notice the Cour du Couvent from the street. Between two cheap clothes shops is a hand-painted sign, a little cracked, reading *"Ébénistes"*. Beneath is a narrow passage, at the end of which the greenery of a little potted garden beckons you. You venture in, and at the end of the pretty passageway is a workshop. Plants are covering the lower half of the window but through it you can see a man in a leather apron polishing a tiny console. It could almost be a scene from the 17th century.

THE SECRET ATELIERS OF PARIS

At one time the Faubourg St-Antoine and its passageways were filled with *ébénistes*, and 12,000 craftsmen in total worked in the *quartier*. Alain Foisy is one of the few who remain. He learnt his trade from his uncle and works with an equally skilled varnisher and an apprentice to his craft, restoring and occasionally reproducing the furniture of the Louis XIV to Louis XVI eras. He has a loyal clientele of antique dealers who know they can trust his exquisite craftsmanship, and private collectors, too, come to him through word of mouth.

Sometimes he works on the same pieces as his neighbour Gérard Brucato – an even rarer species in that he claims to be the last hand-turner in Paris. "It's a case of supply and demand," he says. "There is still quite a lot of call for *ébénistes*, but hand-turned table legs are a rarer request. I have ended up doing some quite unusual commissions, including making wooden jewellery for couture shows and hat stands."

M. Foisy, softly spoken and unfazed by our sudden disruption to the rhythm of his work, is stoical about the disappearance of his craft. "People no longer buy furniture for life, but it is not just mass-production that has killed it. People simply have less furniture. In our grandparents day in a bedroom you would have a bed, a wardrobe, a dressing table, a bedside cabinet. Now what do you have? A fitted wardrobe that serves all purposes. Society evolves."

It is fitting that he works with Louis XIV furniture, as it was the Sun King who established the Faubourg as the centre of the French furniture industry. Versailles was his showground, a precursor to the Great Exhibitions, and when foreign dignitaries came they would be shown the wonderful French craftsmanship and encouraged to place orders for imports. The district still has a visible emphasis on furniture, but most of the shopfronts along the rue du Faubourg St-Antoine itself now sell reproduction Third Empire styles, outlandish leopardskin sofas and ceramic sphynxes or futons imported from Japan. Those artisans who remain are secreted down passageways whose romantic names recall another age.

Michel Fey's family worked on the rue du Faubourg St-Antoine for three generations, but six years ago he moved his leather business to the Viaduc des Arts. Here, under the arches of the old viaduct over which trains once spirited his finished work away to the provinces, 46 craftsmen's studios were created at the time that the Opéra Bastille was built. Michel Fey is clearly willing to move with the times, and the new ateliers are far more of a showcase for the work of the artisans. Filling the large glass window are sturdy leather boxes, chests of drawers and contemporary leather-covered furniture, but behind the plethora of different coloured skins hanging up craftsmen use traditional methods and 200-year-old tools to emboss gilded patterns into leather desktops.

The Viaduc is a fascinating meeting of old and new. Its residents range from a flute and a violin maker through the ancient art of *passementerie* (traditional tassel-making) to a contemporary wrought-iron worker and a creator of delicate wall sconces that take a traditional form and make it modern. There is even the couture fabric house, Malhia Kent. Here fabric designers work years ahead of even the fashion designers, studying predictions and creating exclusive fabrics for the likes of Chanel and Dior. Some of the workshops sell to the trade only, while at others you can watch the creative process and buy pieces too. But all the of artisans who work here seem only too happy to chat for a little while about their craft.

Walking between the Viaduc and the rue du Faubourg St-Antoine, one passes a business that is perhaps an indicator of the district's health. In the window of L. Laverdure & Fils are jars containing exotically named substances – *Pulvis aristolochiae, Aingibar Album, Pulvis absinthii V.* They are neither medicinal, nor the raw materials of alchemy, but pigments used in *ébénisme*.

Above the ateliers of the Viaduc des Arts, running the length of the viaduct, is the Promenade Plantée, a delightful walk that takes you from the Bastille to the Bois de Vincennes. The walk is at its best in June, when the roses lining the route are in bloom.

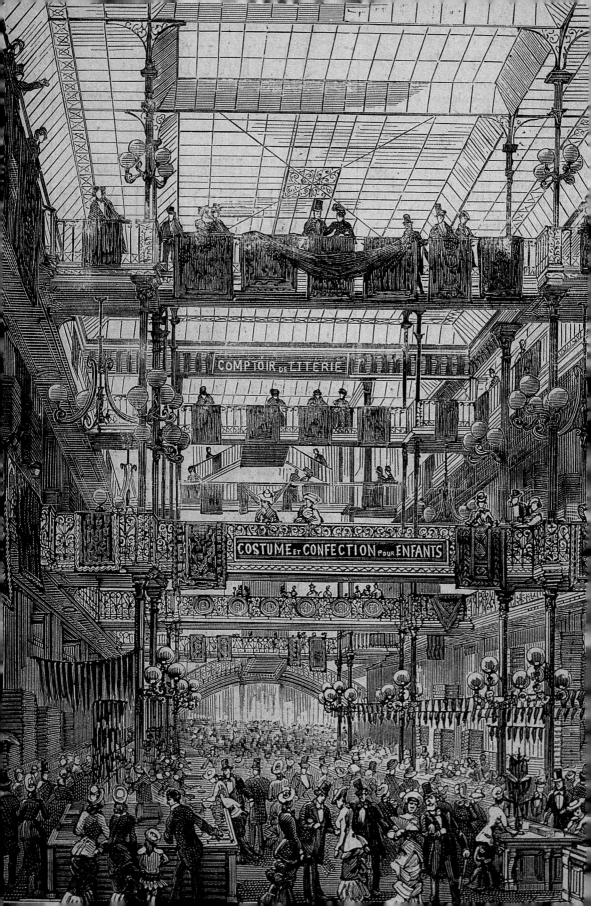

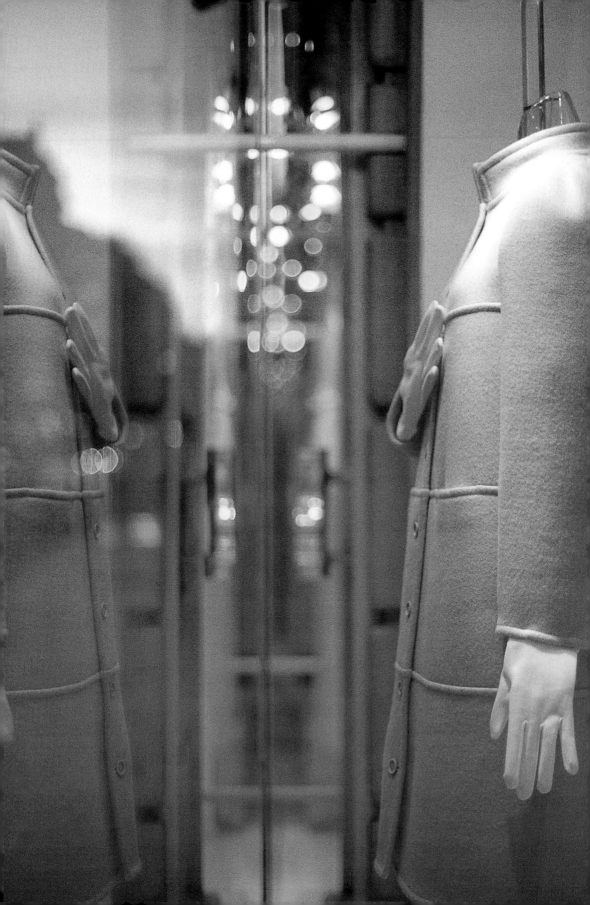

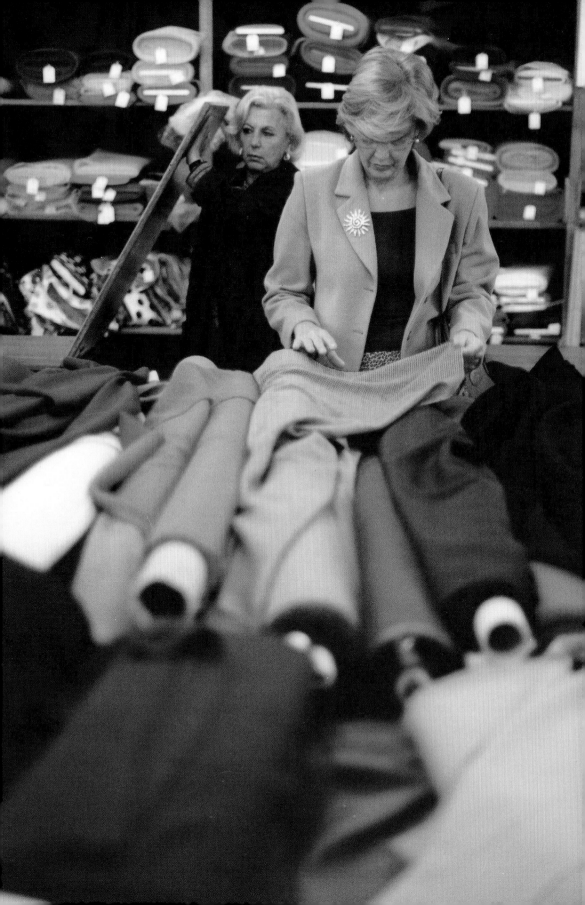

GASTRONOMIC

In Paris, eating is theatre, sustenance and an emotional

PLEASURES

Periodically one hears the cry, "Paris is no longer the gastronomic capital of the world." No city can rest on its laurels, and in this age of fusion food and international tastes the choice of cuisines in Paris may not be as cosmopolitan as in some cities, but only because French food is so highly prized in itself. Pride plays a strong part in the gastronomic life of the capital: cooking is an art where the search for perfection is carried to exquisite lengths, and to eat in one of the top half dozen restaurants is an experience that lingers, like the memory of a wonderful orchestral performance or a fabulous painting seen for the first time.

Eating out first became fashionable in Paris in the first half of the eighteenth century, during the restoration of the monarchy. In that elegant time, when the Palais-Royal was at the height of its fame and Paris attracted large numbers of foreign visitors, restaurants such as Chez les Frères Provençaux, the arcaded Chez Véfour and Maison d'Or in St-Germain, were considered among the finest in Europe: the critic Grimod de la Reynière (1758-1838) even went so far as to call Paris "the best place in the universe for eating well". Other restaurants of that era, such as La Tour d'Argent, still exist; but to discover what comes out of their kitchens is far from a nostalgia trip. Chefs always strive to bring something new, to discover an elixir hitherto untasted and to work ever closer to the seasons and the *terroir*. Of late, even "fusion" has made an appearance, and chefs like Pascal Barbot of l'Astrance show how it really should be done.

journey all rolled into one.

But food in Paris isn't just about *haute cuisine* and restaurants that are the talk of the town. In a country where everyone, no matter from what social class, age or background, can talk for hours on the subject of food, eating well is not just for special occasions. Bistros contain some of the best food in Paris, with young chefs enjoying the freedom of running their own show, taking flight with imaginative variations on classic dishes. Even some cafés have sufficient pride in what they do to offer simple dishes beautifully prepared, home-made desserts and a good selection of tasty cheeses.

The city's specialist food shops and markets are a treat not to be missed, and it is worth taking a day out to explore them. While the established food emporia such as Fauchon and Le Nôtre have a mind-boggling array of goodies that you will long to take home, smaller shops can be rewarding too. Take the time to chat to the owners and taste their produce, finding out a little about the different regions and specialities – no proprietor will begrudge time spent discussing food. And don't forget the sweet delights – no one, but no one (not even the Belgians, in some people's opinions) makes chocolate quite like the French.

"*Haute cuisine* is the difference between *bon* and *fin*. Occasionally someone has come up to me at the end of a meal and said, "That surpassed even my mother's dish." That is the finest compliment you can ever receive because that is the cooking of the heart."
Guy Martin, chef.

THE CRÈME DE LA CRÈME

It is 9.30am. A light mist hangs over the gardens of the Palais-Royal. The Grand Véfour restaurant is serene, its pretty Belle Époque mirrors reflecting the pale morning light over empty tables, yet downstairs the clinical white kitchen is a scene of intense activity. Copper vats are simmering with soups and sauces, sous-chefs bustle round stirring, seasoning and chopping on marble slabs. Huge sacks of rice are delivered. On the wall are lists of spices and the typed descriptions of eight dishes with all their accoutrements – these are the work of Guy Martin, who since 1991 has been chef at this prestigious and almost too beautiful restaurant.

The Grand Véfour epitomizes the *haute cuisine* experience – elegant and intimate surroundings, service that is attentive yet discreet and each dish a subtle marriage of well-chosen ingredients that leaves you searching in your taste memory: what exactly is that elusive flavour that lifts this langoustine, this sea bass or this duck breast into something extraordinary?

The art of eating also means being in a certain place at a certain time in history because *haute cuisine* is always in movement, embracing influences from diverse sources, following its own mysterious rhythm. While luxury ingredients are still the essentials for much of the menu (after all, where else could you indulge in a meal where the starter alone costs more than a meal for two in a bistro?), the *foie gras*, the lobster, the truffles and caviar are now being joined by some daringly plebeian intruders, notably at Le Pré Catalan and at L'Arpège, where Alain Passard's new *haute cuisine* is based on vegetables and seafood.

Universally acknowledged as the most adventurous chef working in *haute cuisine* today is Pierre Gagnaire, whose minimalist dining room sets off such imaginative dishes as *bok choy* with

foie gras and a rooster's *sot-l'y-laisse*, and a risotto of frogs'
legs. Gagnaire takes the approach of encouraging diners to
appreciate his creativity to the full with a *menu dégustation*: a
procession of small but perfectly formed dishes cleverly leading
one into another that show how various international influences
can be melded into a symphonic whole. Even *le grand dessert*
comprises seven separate preparations.

At Guy Savoy's restaurant the eight-course *menu prestige*
similarly demonstrates the range of the kitchen. Savoy's contemporary approach is based on French classic cuisine but with
a lighter touch and includes such seasonal delights as *suprême
de volaille de Bresse* stuffed with *foie gras*, artichoke heart and
truffle, and *langousine éclatée* with coconut and broccoli.

Some of the finest restaurants are now to be found in hotels.
At the Ritz's L'Espadon you dine under a Titian-style painted
ceiling to the sounds of harp and violin music, while Alain
Ducasse's dining-room at the Plaza Athénée, a post-modern
pastiche of Louis XIV by Patrick Jouin, features chandeliers
sheathed in organdie and stark white tablecloths lit by spot-
lights. Le Meurice, Les Ambassadeurs at the Crillon, Le Bristol
and Le Cinq at the Hôtel Four Seasons George V all offer fine
dining experiences in the highest class of hotel. In such perfect
surroundings one feels in the spotlight too, at the centre of
a ballet, as *amuse-bouches* and other tiny offerings form
entractes between courses; even an infusion, should you order
it in place of coffee, is a ritual of measured elegance.

Curiously, *haute cuisine* is an egalitarian experience: it makes
no difference whether you are the toast of Paris or enjoy such a
meal only once or twice a year. The food is king, and appreciation
of it is what matters. In the very best restaurants, even if you
choose the inexpensive lunchtime menu, you will be treated
with the same seriousness and courteousness as the evening's
high rollers. But what about Paris' obsession with seeing and
being seen? The "fashion restaurant" has become as much of
a draw to international visitors as the Louvre or the Centre
Pompidou, a movement that owes much to two men, the Costes
brothers, whose formula of Jacques Garcia design and a fusion
food menu seems to succeed every time.

A newcomer to the
scene, and perhaps the
first foreign chef to
make it into this coveted
élite, is Hiroyuki
Hiramatsu with his tiny
eponymous restaurant
on the Île St-Louis.
Hiramatsu's cuisine
shows the obvious but
hitherto untapped
parallels between the
Japanese and French
love of perfection
in produce and
presentation, his dishes
an uncalorific tribute to
French *haute cuisine*.

Paris' ability to produce
the finest cuisine in the
world is partly due to
the Revolution. After
1789 the highly trained
cooks of aristocratic
families found
themselves without
a job, so opened up
establishments of
their own.

PARIS' BEST RESTAURANTS

For haute cuisine:

L'Espadon

To walk over the thickly cushioned carpets beneath the Murano wall sconces and lavishly swagged windows is to enter a realm of extreme luxury – but this is the Ritz, after all. With the return of chef Michel Roth the sumptuous room is once again the home of some of the finest dining in Paris. In summer the statue-strewn courtyard is a romantic retreat.

Le Grand Véfour

Come here for the elegant, evocative setting (this restaurant was already pulling in a fashionable crowd in the 1830s) and for Guy Martin's subtle use of spices with traditional French ingredients. Afterwards, wander through the arcades of the Palais-Royal.

La Tour d'Argent

The fabulous view of Notre-Dame from this Left Bank eyrie has been enjoyed by Chanel, Cocteau, Bogey and Bacall, and the Queen of England. Duck in blood sauce is the signature dish, the sauce prepared at the table, with silver utensils.

L'Arpège

Approach the vegetable and seafood-based *nouvelle cuisine* of Alain Passard with an open mind and you may find yourself relishing the purity of dishes such as sea urchins with nasturtium flowers and leaves, or scallops wrapped in bay leaves served on a bed of young leeks.

Alain Ducasse at the Plaza Athénée

Under Jean-François Piège, Alain Ducasse's distinctive approach is undiluted and the result is perfection. Seasonal menus build a five-act structure on the theme of the truffle or asparagus. Desserts are sometimes tongue-in-cheek, such as mini brioches which you are forced to dip in chocolate with your fingers!

Lucas Carton

The art nouveau interior with its mirrors, wooden partitions encasing butterflies and plum *banquettes* make this restaurant one of the most beautiful settings in Paris. Alain Senderens' cuisine (interpreted by chef Frédéric Robert) is adventurous, bringing hints of exotic lands. The *millefeuille* is to die for.

Pierre Gagnaire

In minimalist surroundings, with gleaming wood and table-top pebbles for company, take a walk on the wild side with Gagnaire's exuberant menu. It's a dizzying experience.

Le Pré Catalan

The Bois de Boulogne setting is incredibly romantic, and relaxed too, as befits the bucolic location. Frédéric Anton's trademark is dishes that take a single ingredient – *"la carotte"*, *"le pigeon"* – and prepare it in such a way as to enhance its qualities.

PARIS' BEST RESTAURANTS

For being seen:

L'Esplanade

The marriage of restaurateurs the Costes brothers and designer Jacques Garcia accounts for many of Paris' fashionable haunts. Here the Invalides setting attracts a more mature crowd for a menu ranging from Japanese dishes to *sole meunière*.

L'Astrance

Chef Pascal Barbot caused a stir when he opened this restaurant in the 16th in 2001. Grey walls and a metallic ceiling are matched by chic minimalist dishes that draw on his experience cooking in Sydney. Here fusion cooking is all it should be, and more.

Georges

Exceptionally beautiful staff grace the Centre Pompidou's rooftop restaurant with its brushed aluminium pods, translucent tables that glow at night and Philippe Starck cutlery. The usual globetrotting suspects appear on the menu – gazpacho, seared tuna, ostrich steak – but the view is the real point.

Maison Blanche

Revived by the Pourcel twins, who made their name with their Michelin-starred restaurant in Montpellier, this rooftop establishment has slick decor and equally smart waiters. The dishes look great on the plate and taste as good: sea urchins stuffed with dressed crab and garnished with caviar; roast duck fillet with a *pastilla* of carrots and apricots in a spiced sauce. Desserts are fabulous and there is a good selection of Languedoc-Roussillon wines.

Market

Owned by film director Luc Besson, and with African wood and stone décor by Christian Liaigre, Market offers an inventive menu courtesy of chef Jean-Georges Vongerichten: delicious scallops marinated in citrus juice and garnished with roast peppers, potato and *chèvre terrine* with rocket *jus*, lobster with Thai herbs, or crispy duck *confit* with tamarind sauce.

Spoon, Food and Wine

When it opened, this original concept by Alain Ducasse was described as having the effect of "a fire alarm going off in a waxworks museum". Its mix and match of flavours from all over the world has been a huge success.

Bon

Philippe Starck's first restaurant, in the smart 16th, has a fantasy décor of distorting mirrors, candelabras and glass clocks – just what you might expect from the undisputed king of French design. Chef Jean-Louis Amat has brought a south-western touch to the cuisine with dishes like fresh oysters accompanied by tiny grilled sausages, scallops steamed with seaweed and skewered eel with artichokes.

Tanjia

There are many good Moroccan restaurants in Paris, but Tanjia lets you star-spot as you lounge in the chic Moroccan décor and enjoy *tagines* and *pastillas*. Order the mint tea and feign indifference as it is poured deftly from a great height.

Think of your most memorable meal in Paris and you probably don't think of the Tour d'Argent at all, but of that small neighbourhood bistro you ran into on a frosty night where the proprietor sat down and took a glass of *marc* with you and you ate the most delicious *cochon au lait* or rabbit stew. All over the world they try to emulate the Paris bistro, but nobody succeeds. Somehow the checkered tablecloths look fake in New York or London, and the *frites* just aren't the same; and it's difficult to swallow a so-called bistro menu where a mere steak costs as much as a full meal in Paris (not to mention the small carafe of *rouge* thrown in to boot).

BRASSERIES AND BISTROS

However, in recent years something extraordinary has been happening in the world of bistros. While the beloved traditional bistro continues the way it always has been, other examples of the genre are being talked about as their chefs give *haute cuisine* a run for its money. Geniality, tradition and creativity are certainly not mutually exclusive.

One wonders what the Académie Française, determined to stamp out foreign words in the French language, feels about the word 'bistro'. It is, after all, the Russian for "quick". In 1814 the Cossacks were in town, and on account of their hot tempers they were forbidden to enter bars that sold alcohol. Some defied the ban, urging "bistro" in order to avoid getting caught; and this gave rise to a Parisian institution.

For the comfort of knowing that "vielle Paris" still exists, lunch at Chez La Vieille, which has been a bistro since long before the Les Halles market packed off and moved out to Rungis. Old photographs are the only reminder of those days, but the tiny place is full of nostalgia, including the now-rare sound of a rotary phone. Terrines of duck and brawn, *céléri remoulade*, veal braised with green olives and *charcuterie* are homely and filling. Or squeeze into Le Colimaçon in the heart of the Marais, where the two stone-walled, beamed rooms are connected by a spiral staircase so narrow that it seems the waiter has been specially hired for his Giacometti-esque figure and dexterity with trays. In St-Germain, now the realm of Dior and Prada, salvation comes in the form of Au 35, where tweedy publishers and ladies who lunch pile in at midday for simple home cooking. Or there is Thoumieux in the 7th arrondissement whose *cassoulet* is as good as it was in 1923 when it opened – the recipe has been passed down through generations of the same family.

The 12th arrondissement, to the east of Bastille, is rich in good bistros. Le Square Trousseau attracts a media and film crowd whose urban mufti contrasts with the long white aprons of the good-humoured waiters and waitresses. Why do they love it so much? It's not just the absolutely mouthwatering menu but the general atmosphere of *joie de vivre* that ensures that you always leave feeling that a weight has been lifted from your shoulders. South of the Seine the 13th arrondissement, especially the Butte aux Cailles area, has become something of a hotbed of talented chefs, and a chic place to lunch. At L'Avant-Goût journalists and interior designers swap business cards over chef Christophe Beaufront's exquisite yet earthy seasonal menu. His knuckle of pork with slithers of parsnip is divine. Another much talked-about chef is Nicholas Vagnon. His restaurant, La Table de Lucullus, is worth the trip to the 17th arrondissement for dishes such as a *carpaccio* of langoustines, finely dressed *foie gras* and sea bass served with a pepper sauce and purée of lightly smoked aubergines that are far beyond average bistro fare.

Best test of a bistro is its crème brûlée, which should be creamy inside but covered with a thin, brittle sugar glaze that splinters like crystal.

Despite the bistro renaissance, Paris would simply not be Paris without its brasseries. The shiny brass and chrome, the mirrors, the bow-tied waiters bearing aloft plates of seafood and the ice that falls from the outdoor oyster stalls to be crunched underfoot in winter, are a nostalgic part of the Paris experience that can send a little thrill down your neck when you first encounter them. There is a kind of gaudy glamour about brasseries that makes them the perfect place to go for a late-night splurge after the opera or theatre. Yet their origins are ever so humble – they were opened by immigrant Alsatians after the Prussians annexed Alsace-Lorraine in 1870, and originally served up inexpensive *choucroute garnie*, steaks, seafood and salads near the popular shopping streets or in railway stations. La Coupole and Le Dôme in Montparnasse became famous as the haunts of bohemians in the 1930s (as part of the décor La Coupole features frescoes by the artists who were its frequent customers), while Lipp in St-Germain was, and still is, a favourite with film stars and politicos including Lauren Bacall, Jean-Paul Belmondo and François Mitterrand. Many of the brasseries have now been bought up and restored by the Flo group, retaining their distinctive décor and atmosphere, including the Train Bleu, the railway restaurant in the Gare de Lyon.

L'European, opposite the Gare du Lyon, is still a workaday brasserie serving customers wheeling in their suitcases from trains direct from the south of France. Get friendly with the waiter and he might give you a guided tour of the inner sanctums, which include a private room for eight lined in lapiz-coloured glass with Lalique chandeliers.

The sun hasn't yet risen in Paris and already the buttery aroma of freshly baked croissants is wafting from hundreds of bakeries, where *pâtissiers* have been toiling for hours, rolling, folding, turning, rolling, cutting, shaping, waiting. No city is more devoted to good food, and nowhere can you spend a more glorious day simply hunting for edible treasures.

A PERFECT FOOD DAY

Begin at the bakery Poujaran, whose pink bonbon façade brings back childhood sweet shop fantasies. Here, there is nothing routine about the work of baker Jean-Luc Poujaran. He adapts his recipes to the seasons (humidity levels affect the dough's behaviour) and is constantly dreaming up new ways to make his breads tempting. Indulge in a cushiony croissant here – even the politicians at the nearby Assemblée Nationale can't resist them – but above all don't pass up on his *petits pains*, which burst with figs, raisins, apricots, hazelnuts or sweet shallot jam. At lunch, these will make the most flattering accompaniment to fresh and aged farmers' cheeses from Marie-Anne Cantin.

A prominent figure on the Paris food scene (she has founded an association to defend raw-milk cheese), Cantin knows that fine cheese begins with the diet of the goats, ewes and cows that produce the milk – fresh grass produces cheeses that make you think of buttercups, nuts and herbs. She seeks out passionate producers from France and neighbouring countries, and ages their cheeses in her own cellars, separate, pungent rooms for goat's, cow's and blue cheeses. Upstairs, in her gleaming boutique off the rue Cler, a market street, the cheeses are lovingly laid out on straw mats. Crackly orange mimolette, sharp yet creamy roquefort, vacherin so soft you can eat it with a spoon – the choice is up to you, but why not have them all?

A bread and cheese picnic wouldn't be complete, of course, without wine, which gives you an excuse to visit the Bon Marché's luxury supermarket, La Grande Épicerie. Laid out in islands, it's a rather dizzying experience , but let your senses lead you towards a pistachio-studded *pâté en croûte* or precious slices of Spanish Jabugo ham. Pick out some seasonal fruit to end your meal, perhaps slender *gariguette* strawberries in the spring, perfumed white peaches in midsummer or musky grapes in the autumn. Then head for the neatly laid out wine section where helpful staff will find a bottle to match your budget, from a glinting Chablis *premier cru* to a cheerful red Fitou. You're ready to spend a lazy lunchtime in the Jardin du Luxembourg, savouring your feast before the timeless spectacle of graceful statues, groomed lawns and gallivanting children. If you can, supply yourself, as the French would, with china plates, wineglasses and real cutlery – food is a serious business, after all.

Beautiful as it was, that lunch – and the snooze that followed – has left you with a craving for something sweet. If chocolate is your chosen vice, you can't do better than the *pâtisserie* Pierre Hermé, whose sleek dark wood décor makes it look like yet another jewellery shop in this chic district. Indeed, the cakes themselves are jewel-like, nearly all of them some variation on chocolate – the ultimate is *la cerise sur le gâteau*, a pyramid-shaped, layered chocolate cake topped with a cherry. But if ice cream speaks louder than these words, stroll instead to the Île St-Louis and join the queue at Berthillon, whose sorbets (try bitter cocoa with tangy passion fruit) and ice creams (vanilla remains the most popular) may be the most intense in the world.

No food-lover's pilgrimage to Paris would be complete without a visit to the place de la Madeleine, where the famous food halls Hédiard and Fauchon stand proudly side-by-side. Hédiard, the more intimate of the two, was the first to bring exotic fruits such as bananas and pineapples to rich Parisians. Today it remains a source of rare, fragrant spices and evocative fruits from distant lands, as well as unusual teas and coffees, oils, mustards and jams. Fauchon, the grand dame of Paris food shops, will dazzle you with its size and variety – this is the place to put yourself in the hands of expert *traiteurs* who will supply your evening meal of dainty canapés followed by *salmon koulibiac*, lobster in mayonnaise or whatever else strikes your fancy (just don't forget the champagne). A balcony with a view would be a fine place to enjoy this finale – but, better yet, take the staircase near Notre-Dame to the amazingly quiet paved banks of the Seine, where roving musicians will serenade you while passing *bâteaux mouches* light up your meal.

Picnics by the Seine have become an integral part of summer social life, and Mayor Bertrand Delanoë decided to celebrate the fact with his Paris Plage initiative in 2002. Four beaches, 300 deckchairs, 150 parasols and 80 palm trees were imported, bringing the south of France to the capital, and it looks set to be a regular feature for the hot July and August months.

Don't leave the villagey Île St-Louis without visiting L'Épicerie de l'Île St-Louis, a gift shop crammed with jams, mustards, teas, coffees and brightly coloured sugars flavoured with rose or lemon.

The French make uneasy city-dwellers, needing as they do constant reassurance that the countryside, and more precisely the *terroir*, is never far away. Thank heavens, then, for markets, which bring a breath of the provincial to town and keep the seasons turning in terms of colour, taste and smell. Paris has an amazing 85 markets, 73 of which are for food. Some are covered, others are daily outdoor markets and still others are roving: these last are the most extraordinary of all because of their transient nature.

FOOD MARKETS

Every Wednesday afternoon around 3pm at the place du Guignier in the 20th arrondissement, the clanking of poles heralds the unloading of the metal supports for the stalls. These are placed in little holes in the ground at lightning speed and left overnight. In the morning the fruit and vegetables are unloaded in darkness and the market is ready for its customers by around 9am, heralded by the growing mania of the traders as each tries to shout his neighbour down. Here the marketeers are mainly North African and make fun of each other with their exaggerated "Chava?" for "Ça va?" Between the stalls it is pandemonium, old ladies with headscarves and trolley bags storming their way through the *mêlée*, marketeers trying to sweet-talk girls into having a coffee with them while pushing grapes and dates into their hands, babies crying, dogs barking. By 2pm the whole scene has dissolved into a mountain of wooden boxes and trodden-on plums. Then come the *glâneurs*, picking out choice items from what is left behind after the markets are over. The wooden boxes are thrown into a refuse van, the square is hosed down, the poles are taken away, and not a rack remains. Come Saturday the whole process begins again in preparation for the Sunday market.

One of the oldest of the market streets is in the rue Montorgueil – last remnant of Zola's "belly of Paris", Les Halles. Here, with the cobblestones, market stalls and tiny shops filled with hanging *charcuterie*, there is an almost medieval atmosphere. There are pungent cheeses and scent-filled flower stalls, the wonderful Pâtisserie Stohrer and Au Comptoir de la Gastronomie selling *foie gras* and other delicacies.

Some marketeers just want to shift their produce as quickly as they can, while others labour to create beautiful displays. Rue Mouffetard's market in the 5th arrondissement is one of the most picturesque, with tomatoes tied to artificial trees and pretty displays of artichokes, aubergines and spices. It's not the cheapest by any means, but for aesthetic appeal Mouffetard can't be bettered. Between the vegetable stalls there are shops that spill out on the street selling everything you might want for a perfect meal – cheese (there's a very fine fromagerie here with cheese cellars that go right under the road), bread, wine, charcuterie, coffee. On Sundays local people gather to sing forgotten old songs, and other street musicians promote a festive atmosphere that carries on when everyone has adjourned to the cafés.

Less frantically busy and therefore ideal for leisured food-related conversations is the covered market at Aligre, in the 12th arrondissement. This morning-only outdoors North African market sells herbs and exotic fruits, but the covered market stays open all day with butchers, *charcutiers*, a dried fruit stall, a very good Italian deli, flowers and cheese. At the latter you can tell the *fromagier* what day and even which meal you want the cheese for and he will prod and find the perfect example for you, primed to ripen at exactly two o'clock on Sunday. Tasters are given, and advice on keeping the cheeses. Shopping here is really one of the most pleasurable activities in all Paris.

Other markets offer specialities from the different regions of France. Rue Daguerre in the 14th arrondissement attracts a lot of produce from the Aveyron region as well as a superb fishmonger. It's a favourite Sunday morning rendezvous for Montparnassites. Provençal oils and olives are found on Thursdays and Sundays on the boulevard Richard-Lenoir near the Bastille, and *choucroute* and Alpine cheeses at the boulevard Auguste-Blanqui in the 13th arrondissement on Tuesday, Friday and Sunday. There are also three organic markets, the largest (and most chic) on the boulevard Raspail on Sundays, where much of the produce comes direct from the farm.

Many of Paris' suburbs, though they may seem to offer an impoverished version of vibrant city life, have fantastic markets. At sleepy Maisons-Alfort, beyond the Périphérique to the south-east, Saturday sees a huge covered market with rabbits, quail, cockerels with their cockscombs on, octopus, crab and langoustine. The atmosphere is more like a farmers' market, and reminds you that beyond the high-rises of Créteil fields stretch off to the horizon.

"The Parisian takes his chocolate there and his newspaper, his small cup of coffee and his cigar, his mistress, and his ice cream. The provincial takes his lunch and his *National* there, his absinthe, and his wife."
Donald Grant Mitchell, American journalist, 1847.

CAFÉ LIFE

If you closed down all the cafés in Paris the city would probably grind to a halt, so fundamental are they to the life of its inhabitants. In their illustrious history Paris cafés have provided all the essentials of existence, and a little more – food, drink, warmth, company, news, gossip, politics, protection, commerce, philosophy, sex. Hemingway, Sartre and de Beauvoir went to cafés to work, stretching out a *café au lait* all morning to escape the freezing conditions in their own digs in cheap hotels. But central heating seem to have done little to diminish the appeal of cafés – these days in the Café Charbon on the rue Oberkampf earnest young Americans can be seen working on their laptops. At the Web Bar, a 400 metre-square Internet café in an old jewellery workshop designed by the Eiffel studio, computers have not been allowed to erode the human pleasures of talking over a *casse-croûte*, and there are musical and literary soirées too.

Cafés started, as elsewhere in Europe, with the introduction of coffee in the 17th century. In the curious way that foods have of influencing world events, the coffee houses and the heated debate they fostered were a major catalyst of the French Revolution. Throughout the 19th century, aristocrats and the wealthy bourgeoisie would make daily visits to the cafés around the Grands Boulevards – the Café Riche, Café Anglais and Café de la Paix, to discuss politics and parade the latest fashions. But the cafés also had a seedy allure that proved irresistible to the likes of Flaubert and Zola. It was here, in the "first flare of the gaslamp", that courtesans like Zola's Nana hurried, with their skirts held up. As soon as they reached the boulevards they would let drop their magnificent petticoats and parade in front of the cafés, sometimes entering, joking with the waiters and flirting with the men at the tables. The Café de la Paix is still the grande dame of place de l'Opéra, but you pay dearly for the privilege of sitting at one of its tables.

Debate and philosophy in cafés continued with Sartre – the Flore and the Deux Magots were his cafés, the former installing a special telephone line for the existentialist guru. Fifty years on, the tradition has been revived with "café philo", evenings given over to philosophical discussion that are popular with Francophones and Anglophones even though the atmosphere, with a microphone that is handed round for contributions to the debate, is like a rather bizarre form of intellectual karaoke. However, despite its fame the Flore has not lost its appeal to Parisians writers, intellectuals and film-makers – Rive Gauche die-hards Bernard-Henri Lévy and Eric Rohmer are regulars. A different atmosphere is found at the bohemian Maroquinerie in the heights of Ménilmontant, where one's afternoon glass of *rosé* may suddenly be interrupted by earnest debate on such alarming subjects as "France and colonialism".

Cafés in Paris take every form from smart and contemporary to art deco to workaday market bars that haven't changed since the '50s. For authentic café atmosphere where you still find a *zinc*, thick expresso cups, clouds of smoke and a tiled floor it is hard not to fall in love with Le Petit Fer à Cheval on the rue Vieille du Temple. At the front, people perch on stools with their *pastis* and chat to the barman round the horseshoe-shaped bar, while the cosy back room is the place to indulge in big plates of *charcuterie* and hearty daily specials like veal stew and *confit de canard*. In the summer grab a seat on the street and watch the Marais go by. La Coquille near Les Halles is another tiny but atmospheric café run by a Portuguese couple, where you will be served a perfect *kir* or a glass of champagne for less than a coffee at the Flore. Bar du Marché is a perennial favourite with the St-Germain in-crowd, as much for its superlative people-watching as its consistently good service by waiters in dungarees. Order a *kir* and you will be asked which of three wines you would like it made from, and food comes with delicious green salads. A completely different mood is found at Au Vieux Colombier, crowded and chic with carved art nouveau wood and tiny tables where at lunchtime you have to balance your dishes one on top of the other – perfect for an après-shopping apéritif.

Order a *café* and you will invariably get a cup of strong espresso. A *crème* or a *grand crème* are perfect first-thing-in-the-morning coffees, providing creamy sustenance, but there is a third type of coffee known only to the French – the *noisette*. This combines the best of both worlds – the strength of the espresso with a dash of milk. Most traditional cafés don't mind if you buy a croissant at the nearest bakery and eat it then and there on their pavement terrace, along with the coffee you have ordered.

SEASONAL

Paris is a city for any season. Its calendar of events

HIGHLIGHTS

Paris' festival tradition goes back a long, long way. It recalls not only the great religious festivals such as the medieval fair at St-Denis, an enormous, chaotic affair where prostitutes and mountebanks flouted their wares alongside sellers of religious relics, but also the spectacles staged by the monarchy and aristocrats – jousting, masques and fireworks which kept them and the populace entertained. Somehow the revolutionaries knew that Paris wasn't going to forget how much fun it used to have, so new *fêtes* and celebrations were invented to replace the old.

The inumerable trade shows and salons also go far back in history. Louis XIV showcased the manufacturing and fashion industries he had started by sending travelling shows round Europe and inviting foreigners to see the wonders of French craftsmanship at Versailles. This tradition continued after the French Revolution in the form of the great exhibitions of the 19th and early 20th century and these have their modern form in the *salons*, showing anything from yachts to wedding dresses, at the huge exhibition halls on the outskirts of Paris.

For the smart set, the social season follows its immutable rules. The *haute couture* collections start the year in January with a flurry of activity as film stars, socialites, buyers and journalists flock to see the latest creations that have been kept under wraps. Hotel lobbies are frenetic with activity, restaurants have to turn away bookings and taxis suddenly become an endangered species. Within a week the parade is over, only to begin again with the *prêt-à-porter* collections.

guarantees a festive atmosphere whenever you visit.

January also brings the first of the race meetings in the social calendar, the Prix d'Amérique at the Hippodrome de Paris-Vincennes. Later in the year Longchamps and Chantilly will once again be the scene of flamboyant hats and plenty of champagne.

Outside the sporting year, there are plenty of other red-letter days. Saints and sinners all have their fête, from Easter and Whitsun to Bastille Day. Parades fill the streets and everyone, including the Paris *pompiers*, has a ball.

Arts lovers can take their pick from the free Fête de la Musique to the high-brow Festival d'automne. There's jazz in the park, open-air cinema and the delightful Chopin Festival in the Jardins de Bagatelle. Visiting artists at all these events are of a high calibre, making it all the more astonishing that most of the events are free. Running parallel are the many circuses that come to Paris, from traditional shows with trained horses and a ringmaster to the exciting *nouveau cirque* that has found its spiritual home in avant-garde, off-beat Paris.

Meanwhile, the true seasons and their produce come to town in the form of agricultural fairs and the various food salons – mushrooms, truffles, chocolate, all have their day, as does the Beaujolais Nouveau and the wines of other regions at the grand Foire aux Vins. Need an excuse to break open a bottle? Read on.

"Haute couture consists of secrets whispered from generation to generation."
Yves Saint Laurent

THE COLLECTIONS

For two weeks of the year, in January and in July, the fashion world holds its breath as a drum-roll announces the beginning of the couture shows. As exacting, as magnificent and as rarified as the finest trapeze act, couture still sets the style for the rest of the world. Ever since Balenciaga closed in 1967 people have been whispering that "couture is dead", and the recent bowing out of Yves Saint Laurent provoked an almost hysterical flow of nostalgia. But the huge amount of publicity generated by the shows seem to suggest that couture has a few years left in it as the tightrope continues to be walked with an ever-smaller, but consequently richer, clientele. Many of the major houses are now propped up by such giants as LVMH, but in recent years the artistry has been revived by the procurement of young foreign designers such as John Galliano for Dior, and Alexander McQueen for Givenchy – not a new idea: the first real couturier was, after all, an Englishman, Frederic Worth. No matter what the information superhighway can do, or to what extent the market is dominated by American clients (they account for around 60 per cent of couture sales), Paris is and ever will be the epicentre of fashion.

Parisians and foreigners living in the city in the '50s still talk of getting their clothes made by *petits mains*, the trainee seamstresses of the big fashion houses such as Dior or Balenciaga. There are still some 2,200 workshop seamstresses working in Paris *haute couture*.

It all started in the reign of the Sun King, Louis XIV, when the fashions of the court were advertised to the rest of the world by a travelling dress stand dubbed the "doll from the rue St-Honoré". The doll was followed by a retinue of French craftsmen, perfumers, wigmakers and pomade manufacturers, to the great indignation of foreign governments and craftspeople. But no one could beat the Parisians. Neither the Revolution not the Occupation succeeded – in World War II, couturiers Lucien Lelong and the defiant Mme Grès managed to convince Goebbels that a concept as exclusively Parisian as that of *haute couture* could not be developed anywhere but in Paris.

It was Worth who started the idea of having his collections exhibited on live models. Clients such as the Empress Eugénie could watch how the dresses shimmered and moved before placing their orders. Collections became formalized at the end of the 19th century as a way of protecting against rampant plagiarism. The first shows were trade only, and the journalists who attended the shows would sketch Paris fashions for such magazines as *Vogue*, to be consumed by voracious Americans and Brits who would then rush to their own dressmaker with instructions to copy the Parisian ideal. By the 1950s, the absolute heyday of *haute couture*, collections were still a small-scale affair, with only 300 people or so being invited to the first, exclusive *défilé* in the maker's own smart residence or in outlandish settings such as the Eiffel Tower.

These days you can watch the *prêt-à-porter* shows night and day on a 60-inch screen in your suite at the Plaza Athénée hotel, and 1,000 people at a time crowd into the smartest hotels or the Carrousel du Louvre to see one of the 18 elite fashion houses' prototypes. In the front row modern-day beauties such as Gwyneth Paltrow and Sophie Marceau take the place of the likes of Sarah Bernhardt, personalities who could make a designer's season by being seen to wear their clothes in the right places.

Haute couture, however, is still a rarified and magical world. Contrary to the industrial-scale oomph of the *prêt-à-porter* shows, couture collections are minutely stage-managed and afford a dramatic and rarified style of presentation that befits the perfection of the creations. When a client places an order they know that every measurement will be carefully guarded, *toiles* made with the same care as everyday clothes, that the fabrics, buttons and adornments will be exclusive to that house and that they are taking part in the making of a living work of art.

The season is now virtually non-existent; the débutantes, countesses and diplomatic wives who would have deemed their twice-yearly visit to the Paris collections a social necessity are a mere chimera of the past. But while there are still clients willing to pay the price of a car or a small pied-à-terre for an evening dress, the exacting art of *haute couture* will continue.

For those entranced by the mystique of *haute couture*, the pukka second-hand shop Didier Ludot is as fascinating, if not more so, than Paris' two fashion museums. Here, in the arcades of the Palais-Royal, three generations of Chanel suits hang one in front of the other; a Balenciaga wedding dress, 1960, shares the window with a Lanvin dress of embroidered crêpe from 1945; Pucci has its own display, echoed in the modern shop windows in the rue de St-Honoré. Didier Ludot's *tour de force* is his little black dress shop across the arcades – perfect, minimal, classic.

The season may not be quite what it was in the jubilant postwar period when Duff and Diana Cooper held their annual lunch at Chantilly between the Derby and the Prix de Diane – still, this race and the Prix de l'Arc de Triomphe remain the most glamorous events in the Parisian social calendar. The former takes place in June, the latter on the first Sunday of October, neatly surrounding the summer when everybody who's anybody takes off to their yacht. It is hard to choose between the two races either in terms of excitement or visual flair. The Prix de Diane is the French equivalent of the Derby, a thrilling flat race held at the pretty course of Chantilly north of Paris, while the Prix de l'Arc de Triomphe is one of the premier races of the world, attracting some of the best horses worldwide and a large crowd of international trainers and race-goers.

SPORTING EVENTS

Many are the Englishwomen who have arrived at a continental wedding wearing a wonderful headpiece only to discover that the French go hatless. Fortunately the same is not true of the races, and some surprisingly flamboyant creations can be seen on a day when even the most *soigné* throw caution to the wind. Gallingly for the English, who seem to think they have the monopoly on hat-wearing at Ascot, Frenchwomen can pull it off with that little bit more style (it's what's known as the Hermès scarf-tying gene). It helps, of course, that the enclosures are often filled with famous faces from the fashion houses on the arms of dapper gentlemen – since Chanel opened her sporty boutique in Deauville the races have always been *à la mode*.

Two winners at Longchamp and Chantilly in the millinery stakes are Philippe Model and Tête en l'Air. The former, now a veteran of the social season, is famous for his exuberant colours and his signature two-tone designs. Young designers Thomas and Anana of Tête en l'Air, on the other hand, still work from bohemian Montmartre, and their attention-seeking designs have included a Bacchus-style overflowing goblet, which caused quite a stir at Longchamp.

Apart from seeing and being seen, the races in Paris have a particularly electric atmosphere because betting can only take place at the racecourse itself. On any Sunday afternoon it is a pleasure to go out to Auteuil, where Hemingway used to make bets for the staff at the Ritz, but especially in the winter, when you hug yourself to keep warm and the horses' breath billows out in clouds. The stands are completely free and from here you are just metres from the race and in the thick of the excitement. It rarely gets too crowded, except during the Grand Steeplechase de Paris, an elegant social event that takes place in May. The major race at the trotting stadium, the Hippodrome de Paris-Vincennes, is the Prix d'Amérique in January, a razzamatazz-filled event that draws huge crowds. Le trot is a working-class passion, and draws plenty of colourful characters from eastern Paris and the suburbs.

Ritziness is not just the preserve of the races. At the French Grand Slam tennis tournament in early June, spotting stars of screen and stage among the crowds packed into the stands at Roland Garros can take the spectators' eye off the ball momentarily even when some of the greatest tennis players in the world compete. Amusingly, the tournament always sparks off a major enthusiasm for the game, which naturally involves the annual exodus to Lacoste to buy new tennis whites before a court in the Luxembourg gardens (the smartest in town) can be booked. France takes its tennis seriously, but not at the cost of fashion.

It goes without saying that football and rugby have their temples and tournaments, but the most French of all sports, cycling, reaches its zenith here with the closing stage of the Tour de France at the end of July. After weeks of feverish coverage by the press as the Tour snakes its way round France, crowds line the streets and the rooftops of the Champs-Élysées for the greatest bicycle race in the world. To see the tiny figures of the competitors, exhausted and exhilarated as they near the finishing line, is a moving experience.

If your thoughts are more towards the Riviera than the Rond-Point, however, don't miss the Salon Nautique de Paris at the Porte de Versailles exhibition halls in early December. Here are all the superboats and floating gin palaces that you could possibly dream of – an ideal antidote to the Parisian winter.

Chantilly's organisers have an eye for the bizarre, inviting the Kazakhs along for the 2002 event. In between the races, Kazakh horsemen hared along the course, standing bareback on their steeds. Yurts were planted among the picnicking groups and everyone wanted one of the embroidered conical hats that looked as though they'd been designed by Jean-Paul Gaultier.

Deeply Catholic yet staunchly secular, the Parisian psyche is hugely paradoxical, but one thing is for certain: nothing is dearer to the heart of Parisians than their right to celebrate. National holidays are such an institution that to limit them would surely start another revolution. Saints days, patriotic celebrations and workers' holidays mean down tools for everyone – except of course for the sellers of flowers and cakes for the festivities. Museums, shops and restaurants close, transport runs to a minimum and Paris *en masse* heads for the country or to picnic along the banks of the Seine.

SAINTS AND SINNERS

Holiday season *par excellence* is the month of May, when May Day, VE Day, Ascension Day and Whit Monday mean an almost weekly holiday. A lovely May Day tradition survives in the giving of fragrant lily of the valley – they are sold on every street corner and florists give themselves over to a snowy white display.

Each religious festival has its own *quartier*. Good Friday is most flamboyantly celebrated at Sacré-Coeur, where a huge crowd follows the Archbishop of Paris from the bottom of Montmartre up the steps to the cathedral, where he performs the Stations of the Cross. On Assumption Day, 15 August, the focus is Notre-Dame, where a procession parades around the Île de la Cité behind a statue of the Virgin complete with flowers and votive offerings. St John the Baptist is fêted in mid-June with fireworks down the banks of the Seine, and All Saints' Day sees cemeteries bloom with flowers in remembrance of the dead. And now, in multicultural France, *les nuits de Ramadan* are just as much part of the seasonal mix, with parties and club nights to celebrate the Islamic festival.

But the biggest celebration of all is Bastille Day. The official highlight on 14 July is the impressive military parade from the Arc de Triomphe to Concorde, watched by the President of the Republic and thousands of Parisians and visitors. But Paris starts partying early – the evening of the 13th has become renowned for its firemen's balls. These started in Montmartre in 1937, and the fearless *pompiers* of the rue du Jour, rue de Sévigny, rue du Vieux Colombier, rue Blanche, rue Carpeaux and boulevard du Port Royal show no signs of abating. With live bands and an atmosphere where everyone, young and old, can join in the fun, the firemen's balls offer the best parties in town, carrying on sometimes until lunchtime the next day and missing the parade altogether. But on the evening of the 14th, the firemen have to be out in force again for the fireworks at Trocadéro, a fantastic but sometimes alarming spectacle where children with firecrackers try to outdo the official pyrotechnics. Those in the know get a vantage view from the top of one of the office buildings on the Champs-Élysées where they can watch the spectacle with glass of champagne in hand.

Although Bastille Day didn't officially become a national holiday until 1880, it has been celebrated in some form since 1790, when the first Fête de la Féderation took place on the Champ de Mars. 30,000 men, women and children laboured day and night to prepare the ground, singing "Ça ira! Ça ira!" and 300,000 Parisians came to watch the military parades, speeches, cannon and a mass for the new regime. During the following years the festivals continued under a procession of different names. With all its pretensions to overturning the old regime the French Republic realized that the people would not want to give up the spectacles that they had become accustomed to in the days of Louis XIV.

These days Paris' *Mairie* puts on perhaps more free festivals than are found in any other city in the world. There's the country-wide Fête de la Musique on 21 June, when the streets and bars of every district spill over with music, from string quartets to Yiddish singers; the Goutte d'Or en Fête, when Paris' Arab and African quarter plays its heart out; the quirky Paris Quartier d'Été, entertaining those who choose to stay in the city over August with theatre, dance, circus and storytelling; Cinéma en Plein Air on the inflatable screen at La Villette; a wonderful month of free jazz in the Bois de Vincennes' Parc Floral, with such big names as Omara Portuondo and Dave Brubeck, followed by a classical festival in the same place; the river festival, Fête de la Seine; Journée du Patrimoine, when the public can see inside historic buildings; and even a Techno Parade. *Liberté*, *Égalité* and *Fraternité* are joined by Festivity as the party goes on, and on.

Pâtisseries are the great beneficiaries of Paris *en fête* and have even added Halloween to their repertoire as a month-long festivity. In early January you will see them stuffed full of *galettes des rois*, a flaky pastry cake, filled with frangipane, in which a tiny charm is hidden. Whoever finds it dons a cardboard crown, becomes king or queen for a day and chooses a consort.

In Paris you can see the strangest things – a giraffe walking lugubriously down the street in the 11th arrondisement? Two camels in tandem, complete with tassels danging from their haughty foreheads? Spend a few hours in the Clown Bar near the Winter Circus and you may well start to think they are putting something in the *pastis*. But for all its starchy graces and intellectual tendencies, Paris simply adores the gaudy world of the circus.

THE CIRCUS

Though part of the appeal of circuses in our imaginations is their seasonal nature (remember waving goodbye to the circus as a child and wondering how many towns in how many countries it would visit before returning?), Paris has gone one further than most cities: it has become the home of circus with its permanent Winter Circus and four other year-round circus venues. The Cirque d'Hiver is one of the most colourful buildings of the Second Empire, built by Hittorf as a bricks and mortar version of a big top. Inside it is atmospheric, with its tiers of red velvet seating, liveried ushers and balloon-like coloured glass chandeliers. Beneath the auditorium even the animal quarters are sumptuously decorated by modern standards. The Cirque d'Hiver is owned by the Bouglione family, Paris' most famous circus dynasty, and is used for a variety of events from world music and dance to private parties. The highlight of the year is the Cirque Bouglione's own spectacle, a glitzy, cabaret-influenced affair that in the past has included an equestrian ballet in water and a recreation of the trapeze from the Charlton Heston film of that name (filmed in the Cirque d'Hiver itself).

Far from being an annual ritual that adults have to endure for the sake of the children, circus in Paris has always held a great mystique and even a hint of eroticism. At the turn of the 20th century audiences were thrilled by the spectacle at the Hippodrome on Boulevard de Clichy of female chariot races and women dressed as Russian princesses on horseback. Performers from the Cirque Fernando, which later became the Cirque Medrano, mixed with the prostitutes and painters of Montmartre, and appear in many of their canvases. The female clown Cha-U-Ka, the negro clown Chocolat, bony trapezists and a tiny acrobat riding a giant stallion pursued in a sexually charged scene by Fernando's leering ringmaster, were all depicted by Toulouse-Lautrec, while Picasso, in his blue period, dwelt on Harlequins, shadowy misfits, even painting himself as one.

Today the big circus dynasties keep the legend alive. The Bouglione siblings, Joseph and Alexandra, run the permanent big top in the Bois de Boulogne, which frequently hosts visiting troupes and a touring circus. Pinder is another generations-old traditional circus, and to the west of Paris is Francis Schoeller's Journée du Cirque where you can learn to be a clown and lunch with the performers. In complete contrast, La Villette has the Espace Châpiteau, a big top space for contemporary circus troupes that highlights imaginative, innovative acts such as Spaniard Carles Santos' circus-opera *Sama Samaruck Suck Suck*, Théâtre du Centaur's mesmerising *Macbeth* performed entirely on horseback, the well-known French troupe Les Colporteurs and avant-garde circus from Cyrk, graduates of the National Circus School. Other big tops pop up spasmodically in locations such as the Tuileries gardens or place du Stalingrad, where artist Daniel Buren, famous for his striped cylinders in the Palais-Royale devised a circus in "rooms" made up of striped cloths and mirrors.

However, one of Paris' most beloved circuses is neither spectacular nor avant-garde, but is found on a bit of wasteland in the 11th arrondissement known as Cité Prost. Romanes Cirque Tsiganès was started by Alexander Romanès (a Bouglione, but only in name) and Délia, the woman he fell in love with on a gypsy encampment at Nanterre. In their tiny, intimate *châpiteau*, they present a family circus that is as raw and emotionally charged as the gipsy music that accompanies it. There are no safety nets here, just Délia, who sings plaintively while holding her arms aloft towards the tiny child who spins on the trapeze. After the performance they serve red wine and home-made doughnuts to an enraptured audience who have been taken far, far away from their daily lives. Then suddenly they'll disappear, with carpets, tent and the scrap metal they use for the trapeze bundled into their caravans, leaving just the memory of their music and their *joie de vivre*.

La Villette's Cabaret Sauvage is a uniquely Parisian venue that combines a big top atmosphere with varied events, from private parties to club nights. At Ramadam it hosts *Les Nuits de Ramadan*, when Moroccan lanterns are suspended from fairy lights – you can dine on *tagine* while Berber women sing and jugglers perform, and dance with the troupe at the end of the evening.

Every year the French press prints the same headline: "The country comes to Paris." It's February and the Salon de l'Agriculture is taking place in the Porte de Versailles exhibition ground. This must be the only European country where the *terroir* comes that close to the people; but, after all, French farmers are not like others – they embrace city-like values of social mobilization in times of crisis, and the cities love them for it. Even more than this, food, real food, is so close to the heart of every French citizen that for them there is no nonsense about loving the product but not its source – seeing nature "red in tooth and claw" is all part of the gustatory experience.

THE FOODIE CALENDAR

At the Salon de l'Agriculture you can prod cattle, talk about goats' milk yield and taste the wonderful products of the soil. No matter how many generations they go back, all Parisians have an uncle or a cousin who works the soil or has a vineyard, and professes to know not a little about the subject.

It is, after all, just in living memory that goatherds still walked the streets of the Left Bank, milking their animals into pails, as recounted by Hemingway in *A Moveable Feast*: "The goatherd came up our street blowing his pipes and a woman who lived on the floor above us came out onto the sidewalk with a big pot. The goatherd chose one of the heavy-bagged, black milk-goats and milked her into the pot while his dog pushed the others onto the sidewalk." And it is less than 30 years since Les Halles ceased to be the meat-market of Paris with all the life and rigour that that entailed.

One is much more aware of the seasons in Paris than elsewhere, not just because the pedestrian nature of Paris life forces you to be in the open air for at least five minutes a day, but because of the obsession with food. A weekly trip to the market reveals that bright red peppers are only really available for one week of the year, and the different types of mandarin change weekly, from the rather spiritless ones of late November to the tight, bright orange ones of mid-December, with their leaves intact.

And the calendar of food fairs goes on. Autumn is the ripest time, kicked off with the *vendanges* in Montmartre itself, where the city's own vineyards are celebrated with a parade from town hall to vineyard and back. Montmartre is one of five urban vineyards – their vintages, let's face it, are no competitor to St-Émilion, but the *vendange* is a wonderful excuse to *fête* the vine and all it stands for in Bercy, Belleville, Parc Georges Brassens and Parc Monceau. City vintners are on hand with advice on pruning and fermentation and *dégustations* of the latest crop, often decorated with an artistically drawn label.

In November, the arrival of the Beaujolais Nouveau is celebrated with all-night drinking and *fanfare* music in restaurants all over town, but serious wine buffs wait for early December when the Foire aux Vins brings major producers to Paris. If you have a cellar – and even the smallest Parisian flat is often equipped with one as part of a subterranean space-sharing arrangement – now is the time to stock up on vintages with the help of *dégustations* and long conversations with producers from all over France. It is second only to taking the trip down to the producers in spring and tasting *en primeur*.

There is a second food fair, the Salon des Fermiers, in October, where all but the actual animals are present. You can certainly see cockerels with their plumes on, taste freshly sautéed Salers beef and have a truly earthy conversation with thick-accented provincial types about the farming of *escargots* or quails.

The Salon du Chocolat is held in the fashion-conscious surroundings of the Carrousel du Louvre, where not only is every gourmet chocolatier in Paris present with fabulous examples of their craft, but there are even fashion shows where the models (who have clearly abstained from chocolate from childhood) sport chocolate dresses and headdresses.

But most dangerous of all is the Salon du Champignon. Even in Paris, the keen head off to the Fôret de Fontainebleau to seek out these tasty but potentially lethal morsels. The salon, held in the Jardin des Plantes, has mycologists on hand to advise on which are actually safe to eat. An alarming number of people are taken to hospital with mushroom poisoning each year, but here at least you are in safe hands when nibbling on a *girolle* or rarer delicacy.

On certain Thursdays you will find a wonderful array of *saucissons secs* and peasant loaves at the Gare du Nord – ideal for those in transit to gastronomically impoverished England. When questioned about the regularity of their visits the farmers gave nothing away, but one Parisian ventured the suggestion that the wily *Auvergnats* were making the most of a train strike by setting their wares out to pass the time most profitably.

AFTER DARK

High-kicking girls are just for show – there is much

While the phrase "Paris, city of lights" was actually coined during the Enlightenment, referring to the philosophical luminaries of the day, it is indicative of this city's unique mix of the intellectual and the hedonistic that the tag has stuck. These days, the city of lights is the city of bars and cafés disgorging their customers onto the pavement, cabarets, theatres and cinemas advertising their shows, tinselly trees filled with fairy lights year-round and the familiar monuments looking stately in their illuminated grandeur.

To drive (or, even better, be driven) around Paris after dark is one of the city's greatest thrills. Engines throb on the Champs-Élysées as you draw up at the traffic lights alongside clubbers eager to lose the week's stresses in a night of hedonism. With the windows down, rival beats fill the air with anticipation. At place de la Concorde you whizz round in a frenzy of movement, passing fountains gushing light, the bright shopfronts of the rue de Rivoli and the dark mystery of the Tuileries gardens. Nothing is more tantalizing than the Seineside crawl past 17th-century buildings lit up like a stage set and the little *péniches* nestling on the water.

In Paris one is not hidebound by opening hours: the *nuit blanche* (staying up all night) is an institution. It is quite possible to sit down to eat at 11pm, especially at the large and welcoming brasseries which are your best bet for a post-theatre feast on oysters and seafood. Thereafter the night is yours. Choose a cabaret, jazz or dancing. If you want to carry on until 11 or 12 the following day you can, before falling into bed after a very large hot chocolate.

more to Paris nightlife than the Moulin and its acolytes.

The legendary names of the Paris nightscape are kept alive, some more authentically than others. There is still the Moulin Rouge, the Lido and the Crazy Horse with their high-kicking girls, and the troglodyte jazz cellars of St-Germain. The latter still beats everyone hands down for its late-night atmosphere, with coffees and *croque-monsieurs* served out on the pavement till whatever time you want and plenty of gossip and people-watching huddled under the orange heating lamps.

But the fashion crowd these days is back on the Élysées and the Faubourg St-Honoré, starting the night with a perfectly mixed cocktail at a hotel bar – the intimate and gentlemanly Hemingway Bar at the Ritz, the fashionably luxurious Plaza Athenée or the more lively and *branché* Costes. Paris has also formed a prototype bar-restaurant concept that no other city has successfully copied – the Buddha Bar, Man Ray and Alcazar, theatrically decorated and lit spaces with wide staircases to make anyone feel like a starlet, they metamorphoze seamlessly from restaurant to club as the tables are cleared away piece by piece to make room for dancing. Then there is another world, far from the label-wearing crowd, where cheek-to-cheek dancing still goes on with the revival of the tango, *merenge* and even the waltz. Sleep, you could say, is as dead as the proverbial "*dodo*" (French for bedtime).

It is one of the peculiarities of Paris social life that one often receives invitations containing the words *autour d'un cocktail* (literally "around a cocktail") and yet on arriving at the function one is only ever offered wine or champagne.

COCKTAILS AT THE RITZ

But if there's anywhere in the world where one should drink a cocktail it is Paris. Between here and New York, and on the transatlantic liners that plied between the two, the finest cocktails in the world were invented. Each encapsulates an era – the gin rickeys and mint juleps of the pre-war years; the Blue Bird, 1933, invented to commemorate Sir Malcolm Campbell's azure-tinted speed machine; the Manhattan, created in the 19th century by Winston Churchill's mother to celebrate Samuel Tilsden's election as mayor of New York City; and the Chambery Fraise, otherwise known as the French martini. A saving grace is found at the end of a very long, glittering corridor entered from place Vendôme – the Hemingway Bar at the Ritz.

It is easy to get Hemingwayed out in Paris, for there is hardly a bar that the writer didn't drink in and recall in his fond, intimate memoir *A Moveable Feast*. But the Hemingway Bar at the Ritz is more than just an idle tribute. In this cosy, wood-panelled temple to the twin deities of Papa Hemingway and the cocktail, one finds the ghostly presence of the writer.

All this is due to Colin Peter Field, the English head barman, who, with his perfectionism, his charm and his passion for his *métier*, has created something quite unique. The Hemingway Bar is very much Field's bar, as it was Bertin's and Frank Meier's before him. Bertin, a neat man with a wry smile and twinkling eyes, was Hemingway's barman and even had his bets placed by the writer, as did many of the Ritz staff. But it was Meier who raised the art of bartending from mixing perfect drinks into being the perfect host.

Field, who keeps his bar free of music – except for the occasional burst from his wind-up gramophone – has an extraordinary memory for Hemingway tales. A favourite is the "orchid trick": "One evening Hemingway was sitting up there and Fitzgerald was sitting in that chair over there and there was a lady sitting

The Ritz is one thing; the perfect Mohito is another. Tiny Calle 24 at the bottom of the Marais is the place, where diminutive Cuban manageress, Mechy, mixes superlative South American cocktails using three-year-old Havana Club. Private clubs are not common in Paris, but Parisians have come to love the atmosphere of Chesterfields and cigar smoke. At the China Club in the 12th arrondissement you'll find a '30s Shanghai ambience, without the need for membership, and the cocktail waiters are top-notch.

about here, and Fitzgerald asks the bartender, I think it was Bertin, to offer a bouquet of orchids to the lady. So Bertin gave the orchids to the lady and she said, what kind of a girl do you take me for, take the orchids back to Mr Fitzgerald. Fitzgerald starts eating the orchids, the lady starts laughing and they end up going out to dinner. So if all else fails, try the orchid strategy."

This is the thing about the Ritz. Anywhere else in the world you'd probably be hard-pressed to find an instant bouquet of orchids, but here, as Field says, "you have the tools to do the job". Thus orchids have become one of his favourite garnishes, along with roses (pink or red according to the lady's colouring and clothing) and even conkers.

Field is one of an elite of four – Salvatore Calabrese in London, Dell de Groff in New York and Charles Schumann in Germany being the other three – whose passion for the art of mixing has taken cocktails into another realm, the drinks equivalent of *haute cuisine*. In this rarified world perfectionism is carried to almost metaphysical heights. The ingredients for the dry martinis are kept in a fridge at precisely -18.4°C. The Ritz makes its own Limoncello – the result of six months' alchemy behind the scenes – and its own version of Southern Comfort, a particular favourite with a foreign prince. New drinks are invented using seasonal and regional ingredients such as lemon verveine (from May to October) and truffles. For the Cognac aux truffes Field waits until the first frosts of February and imports truffles from the Dordogne. "At around 550 euros a kilo of truffles and 20 bottles of X-O you have to have a lot of courage as far as your cost control is concerned. But we did it and we've been out of it for two months. Anyone who tastes it immediately says 'Let me smoke a cigar'. It's just so deep it's fantastic."

He disappears behind the scenes for precisely 45 seconds and returns with two glasses of perfectly chilled vodka, then drops a tiny pipette of blue food colouring into them. The effect is magical, the blue dye making spiral patterns like Murano glass, which slowly diffuse leaving a pale blue tint. "The Blue Princess, created for Van Cleef and Arpels after a diamond that Mr Arpels bought in 1953. Totally pure like the diamond, it's cold like a diamond can be." A diamond, perhaps, as big as the Ritz.

"What do rich girls dream about?"
"Hotel life."
"Which hotels do they like best?"
"They all like the same one best – the Ritz."
"What is the Ritz?"
"It's Paris."
"And what is Paris?"
"The Ritz."
Léon-Paul Fargue's catechism for beautiful women travellers, as recounted to Proust over chilled melon in the aforementioned hotel and reproduced in *Le Piéton de Paris*, 1939.

"IF YOU ARE LUCI

HAVE LIVED IN PARIS

THEN WHER

FOR THE REST

FOR PARIS I

KY ENOUGH TO

AS A YOUNG MAN,
EVER YOU GO

OF YOUR LIFE,

IT STAYS WITH YOU,

A MOVEABLE FEAST."

ERNEST HEMINGWAY, *A MOVEABLE FEAST*

The jazz of Miles Davis, Dizzy Gillespie, Art Blakey and Thelonious Monk is the definitive soundtrack to the Left Bank of the '50s. It even made it onto the *Nouvelle Vague* films of the era. In 1958 Davis improvised to Louis Malle's *L'Ascenseur vers l'Échaffaud* in the Studio de la Poste in St-Germain with Jeanne Moreau herself greeting musicians and technicians at an improvised bar. The music has a spooky, edgy quality that evokes a Paris of frenetic streets and rain and smoky cafés.

JAZZ IN PARIS

Paris' association with jazz started long before, in the jazz age, which the French term *les années folles* (the mad years). This was the era when the surrealists were experimenting with automatic writing, Kiki (lover of Man Ray) was the self-proclaimed queen of Montparnasse, and Le Monocle was the famous Montmartre dance-hall where women dressed as women danced with women dressed as men – in dinner jackets and Eton crops, often sporting the eponymous monocle.

Centre of the action was a little *boîte* called Bricktop's, where virtually every writer, musician and bohemian of the day ended up at some time. Scott Fitzgerald and Henry Miller were regulars. The Duke of Windsor was a friend, and couturier Elsa Schiaparelli financed the club for the Harlem singer nicknamed for her tinted orange hair. Evelyn Waugh, on his way to Monte Carlo in 1929, was waylaid by a party of Americans in Paris and recounts how they made their way around Montmartre, drinking ever more dreadful champagne, and returning habitually to Brickie's only to find that she wasn't opening till four. Eventually he gets in, declares Bricky the "least bogus person in Paris" and goes off to eat soup in Les Halles.

Jazz in Paris has its origins in a climate of liberation that black musicians did not find at home in the US or in London. Josephine Baker met Sidney Bechet on the boat over and her gave her the start that made her one of the most celebrated acts 20th-century Paris ever knew. She shook her banana-clad booty in a way that would be seen as simply shocking today, as well as becoming a Resistance heroine who the French took to their hearts. Jazz was playing in Paris even before World War I had ended, and after the Liberation of Paris at the end of World War II there was another explosion of the music that had been suppressed during the Occupation. Many of the places – the Club St-Germain, the Montana, Le Chat qui Pêche – have now disappeared, but some still remain, notably the Caveau de la Huchette with its authentic cellar atmosphere where people really do boogie-woogie, and the Bilboquet in rue St-Benoît, where Miles davis habitually played. You can also find traditional jazz with subterranean St-Germain atmosphere at L'Arbuci Jazz Club and the Petit Journal St-Michel. But jazz has always been a genre in transit. There is now such a wealth of music crossing all strands of jazz culture that on any night of the week you can take your pick from dixieland to electro-jazz at any number of venues, large and small.

Jazz of the forward-looking variety has moved to the Right Bank. To see free jazz French style, try Le Duc des Lombards, a New York-style corner bar in Châtelet, or Le Sunset and its all-acoustic sister venue Le Sunside. There's also Le Petit Opportun, hosting big French names in a tiny medieval cellar, Le Baiser Salé (salty kiss) for late-night Afro-Jazz and Les 7 Lézards for free-bopping improvisation. Man Ray's mezzanine bar has live jazz nightly till midnight for sipping cocktails to. Jazz barges for swinging and swaying include La Balle au Bond and the Péniche Blues Café. And for electro-jazzers such as Eric Truffaz and Laurent de Wilde you must travel out to the wilds of Montreuil to Les Instants Chavirés.

The *crème de la crème* of jazz musicians as well as world/jazz crossovers are to be found nightly at New Morning, a now legendary venue that was founded by Eglal Farhi, an Egyptian-born former UN worker, just over 20 years ago. Virtually indiscernible from the street, set among Turkish fast-food joints and the edgy neighbourhood off rue St-Denis, the club has an easy-going atmosphere that defies everything you might expect about Paris and about jazz. If there's no room in the auditorium people crowd behind the bar and the bartenders just shrug and smile. You might come to New Morning to hear Herbie Hancock, Courtney Pine or Julien Lorau, but most of all go there to see Parisians visibly having fun – it's infectious.

It was only two years since World War II had ended. Austerity was still a way of life and displays of ostentation could have shocking repercussions, such as when incensed women tore the New Look from the back of a model during a fashion shoot in Montmartre. Yet in 1947 Bernard Lucas opened a cellar bar under the Café Tabou and installed Juliette Gréco, the poet Anne-Marie Cazalis and actor Marc Doelnitz as its muses. Aided only by a gramophone and cheap red wine the trio and their circle forgot the past in a frenzy of jitterbugging and spontaneous jam sessions. It was the spirit of the age, the only place to be after midnight in St-Germain. A month later, instigated by Cazalis, the now-famous article appeared in *Samedi-Soir* exposing the "troglodytes" of St-Germain, who were "drinking, dancing and loving their lives away in cellars until the atom bomb – which they all perversely long for – drops on Paris." Existentialism as a tourist attraction had begun. Sartre was driven from his table at the Flore, mid-western Americans started growing beards and people squeezed into the bars and basements to gawp at the troglodytes.

HOT SPOTS

Fifty years later you can still see them – pale faced, black haired girls smoking aloofly and thin bearded young men – in the Cine-café Le Reflet, and in temporary jazz clubs where men in their twenties try to recreate the sounds of Davis and Parker. But the spirit of St-Germain is one of nostalgia, and you have to look elsewhere for today's Paris Zeitgeist.

Curiously, the city has now become polarized not between Right and Left Bank but between east and west. In the west, the Champs-Élysées has undergone a sparkling revival that would never have been imagined ten years ago. Past the burger bars and pizzerias cruise young men in their BMWs, one hand on the knee of their adoring girlfriends who are practised in the art of walking from kerb to club in Manolo Blahniks. This label-conscious crowd congregates in the incense-filled gloom of Buddha Bar, sipping cocktails insouciantly while looking down on the cavernous dining-room presided over by a huge Buddha. They might move on to Man Ray, Bar Fly or Tanjia, the Moroccan restaurant owned by club impresarios David and

Cathy Guetta, which gave its name to "riad-chic". Or you'll find them at Nobu, the Paris version of the New York and London restaurant whose exquisite Japanese/Peruvian fusion cuisine defies its fashion status. Design fanatics are attracted by Atelier Renault on the Élysées itself. Feeling like a presenter in a '60s newsreel you can wander among futuristic vehicle prototypes and furniture by Philippe Starck, while upstairs a cocktail lounge is suspended from the ceiling by metal rods. And let's not forget the Costes brothers. Whatever they, and favourite designer Jacques Garcia, turn their hand to seems to turn to gold, particularly in the case of neorococo Hôtel Costes in the Faubourg St-Honoré. Here, on the upholstered sofas and armchairs, models, fashion and music faces define the word "lounge".

Zip down the rue de Rivoli, turn left at the Bastille and you will find yourself heading for eastern Paris' hub of bars and nightlife. Known as the "Oberkampf strip", the rues Oberkampf and Ménilmontant glisten with a thousand tiny lights as you look down from the very top of this steep climb. Between here and the Élysées may be only a matter of a few miles but the two worlds scarcely ever meet. Bars like the Café Charbon, an old and atmospheric café-theatre that serves brunch on Sundays and experimental music at night in its industrial-style club, attract artists, young fashion designers and webmasters. The choice of bars along the strip is manifold, but most sport bare brick, squishy velvet sofas picked up in brocantes or collections of kitsch, while party people dance through the night at jazz-funk bar the Cithéa. The area is multicultural, and as you climb the hill you encounter Chinese traiteurs, African wig shops and tiny neighbourhood cafés run by affable Algerians. In a few years no doubt the troglodytes of today will have moved on: already the scene is moving north to Belleville, and there are even hints that Pigalle is due for a revival; but in the meantime bustling Ménilmontant and the glitzy Champs keep the nuit blanche alive while the rest of Paris slumbers.

The musical style of the Champs-Élysées revival has travelled far beyond the 8th arrondissement with the trademark "lounge" CDs of Buddha Bar, Man Ray, Costes et al. But where was the Nirvana Lounge, origin of Buddha Bar DJ Claude Challe's latest offering? In fact, it didn't exist, but Challe became so fed up with people asking that he has made their fantasy reality, opening Nirvana, the bar to match the CD.

While bar-hopping in Oberkampf you may notice peculiar white skeletal figures painted on the buildings and walls. These are the work of artist Jerôme Mesnager, and figures like them, symbolizing "the free human being", can be seen as far afield as New York, Senegal and the Great Wall of China.

The legend of the Moulin Rouge lives on, and on, and on. And if the cabaret today is a hit only with Japanese tourists and Bradford businessmen (do they know, one wonders, that most of the girls are from Yorkshire too?), its spirit will never die. Most recently it sparked the imagination of the Australian film-maker Baz Luhrman with his lurid tribute to Busby Berkeley and Bollywood, starring Nicole Kidman and Ewan McGregor. Everyone has heard of the Moulin and remembers the images from Lautrec's posters. But what was it really like to be in Paris when the red lights of the turning sails first lit, like a beacon, the surreal world of Montmartre with its eery cathedral and steep cobbled streets?

CABARET

By 1889, when the Moulin Rouge was built by Joseph Oller and Charles Zidler as a money-spinner during the Great Exhibition of that year, the real windmills of the *Butte* had long since ceased to turn; but the vulgar red light of this blatantly phoney mill with its mocking moon and sun proved that the innocent world of Renoir's *Moulin de la Galette* was soon to disappear. Aiming to outdo the Élysée-Montmartre, the great dance-hall on boulevard Rochechouart where the *chahut*, or cancan, had begun to the music of Offenbach, Zidler created what was meant to resemble a trip to the Underworld itself. A dance-hall the size of a railway station was filled with the incredible din of an orchestra of trombones, bass drums and cymbals; a garden with little tables had as its centrepiece an enormous cardboard elephant that acted as an orchestra stand; monkeys on chains entertained; and in the gallery the dancers metamorphozed from untouchable performers to courtesans. He even had the audacity to steal the Élysée's best dancers, Jane Avril and La Goulou. The latter, though plump and rather common-looking, commanded great fees at the height of her career and even dared to flip off the Prince of Wales' top hat with her foot as he watched the show.

Other cabarets of the day included the Casino de Paris, now a theatre, and, a little later on, the Folies-Bergère. Le Chat Noir was home to political satire, while L'Enfer provided a trip to hell in the form of women pretending to be whipped and hurled into boiling oil by yelling devils, while waiters dressed as skeletons served undrinkable drinks. The terrifying façade of this building was finally wiped from the scene in the '50s.

All of them have lasted, however, albeit in transmuted form. The Moulin Rouge still serves up the cancan in a feather-filled, Vegas-style spectacle, and has been joined by the Lido, the more intimate Nouvelle Eve and the Crazy Horse with its nude light show. Meanwhile the Élysée-Montmartre is now a huge club where hands rather than feet punch the air as an exuberant crowd dances to house music spun by celebrity DJs. L'Enfer has reappeared as a club in Montparnasse, offering hedonistic parties that start at dawn, and the Chat Noir is reborn as a jazz venue. Picasso's beloved Lapin Agile still exists, providing accordion and traditional French songs, but a closer approximation to the atmosphere in his day can be found at small, snug bars such as Chez Adel and l'Attirail, where musicians pass round the hat and the drinking goes on just as long as the owner can manage to stay awake. But things often go full circle. Now circus impresario Francis Schoeller has bought the old Berry Zèbre cinema in Belleville and aims to make it a new concept in entertainment. It will have trapeze and *chanson*, red velvet and café tables. In fact, it will have, he says, "l'esprit du Moulin Rouge".

At the Casino de Paris not only was cheap music-hall on offer but, in 1900, *a grand manège vélocipede* – bicycle lessons every afternoon. Cycling, for women, was considered quite as immoral as the cancan.

"... IN THIS PLACE NO PASSIONS NEED BE CURBED. THERE IS SHOUTING AND HORSE-PLAY; WOMEN ARE CARRIED ROUND THE HALL ON THE SHOULDERS OF MEN; THERE IS ONE FIERCE INCREASING CRY FOR DRINK. A MAN DRESSED AS A TOREADOR... PASSES ME WITH A WOMAN SITTING ON HIS SHOULDERS. HER ARMS ARE ROUND HIS NECK, HER COARSE FACE IS UNREDEEMED BY ONE SOLITARY SIGN OF EVEN DORMANT INTELLIGENCE."

AN ENGLISH REPORTER SHOCKED BY THE MOULIN ROUGE IN THE MAGAZINE 'PICK ME UP', 1900.

It is Sunday night in the eastern suburb of Montreuil. Behind a plain white door marked *privé* is an industrial building where roughly painted white walls, a deeply slung red velvet curtain and a sprung floor comprise the décor. At the bar, and sitting on a frayed velvet-covered banquette sharing cake and figs, are groups of young people. The girls are imaginatively dressed, some with short dresses over trousers as it is a cold night, fluffy jumpers and little fluffy boas. Then the band – accordion, guitar and double bass – strikes up and they take to the floor, gliding in unison, and turning with flirtatious little heel movements. Some, forehead pressed to their partner's face, look as if they are in a deep trance. Others smile and feign surprise at their partner's choice of direction. This is one of Paris' new tango *boîtes*.

WHERE TO DANCE

The tango came to Paris in the '20s with Frenchmen who had danced it in Buenos Aires brothels, and gradually filtered up into the higher strata of society. In the early years, though, it held a rather louche appeal: La Coupole, in its downstairs ballroom, had one orchestra for tangos and one for blues. In the afternoons older women came here to dance with young men, while the dance was also popular at the Sapphic club, Le Monocle. After the war it was overtaken by high-voltage jitterbugging, but in the '60s a new wave of Argentinian *émigrés* arrived in Paris fleeing political upheaval. While they largely kept themselves to themselves, elements of the tango escaped into the Paris consciousness. (Just listen to the sound of the accordion on the Métro or on the Montmartre pavement – more than likely it will be a tango. On a rare occasion you might be treated to the sound of a real *bandoléon* too.) Now the music is once again in vogue and has entered popular music with Gotan Project, who take old tangos and rework them with a deep bass and sultry electronic mix.

Today's tango boom is largely due to people like Frédérique Behar who fell in love with it when invited along to a soirée by a friend and claims to have danced almost every night since. "I had never really gone to nightclubs, but when I saw this I knew I had to do it," she says. "We dance in places like this, intimate and *chaleureux*, and in the summer on the quais." Her Casa del Tango in the unfashionable 19th arrondissement holds lessons, *bals*, concerts and literary soirées. Tango, for some, is more of a religion than a dance.

Somehow, Paris seems to have an irrepressible need to dance cheek-to-cheek. While the Rex, the Élysées-Montmartre and Le Queen pack in the crowds to rave to euphoric techno music, dancing with a partner still has a huge appeal. The trend for rock-'n'-roll dancing, in which all French teenagers seemed to have been schooled for decades (perhaps by their Johnny Hallyday-loving parents), appears to have died out, but only to be replaced by fast and furious salsa. Parisians have discovered their Latin temperament, and clubs such as Pachanga, the Barrio Latino and La Java heave with muscly young men swinging their partners round in an ever-increasing frenzy. Even La Coupole has caught on and has revamped its basement *bals* as salsa evenings.

Interestingly, another dancing scene that was once dismissed as old-hat has started to see some young faces. On the banks of the Seine and Marne are the *guingettes*, outdoor dance-halls where you can eat lunch or supper then dance a foxtrot, *musette* or even a rock-'n'-roll number to a live band. Chez Gégène at Joinville-le-Pont has been going since the turn of the century, while Le Guingette de l'Île du Martin-Pêcheur at Champigny-sur-Marne was built in the '80s and is reached by pulley-raft. There's also a thriving *guingette* in the middle of Clignancourt market, called Chez Louisette. Evocative of a village wedding at the turn of the century, the *guingettes* are done out in bunting and red tablecloths and serve steak, *moules* and carafes of red wine. On Assumption Day Chez Gégène was in full flow, with dapper elderly couples in shiny shoes and pearls, grandmothers dandling babies and groups of students in their twenties having a ball. Whoever said that dancing cheek-to-cheek was *passé*?

You've heard of singing waiters, but a dancing chef? At Chez Raymonde in the 11th arrondissement you may be happily chomping your way through a steak when the lights dim to pink, a piano and accordion strike up and chef comes waltzing right out of the kitchen into the arms of the host. The diners, of course, join in.

ELYSEE
MONTMARTRE

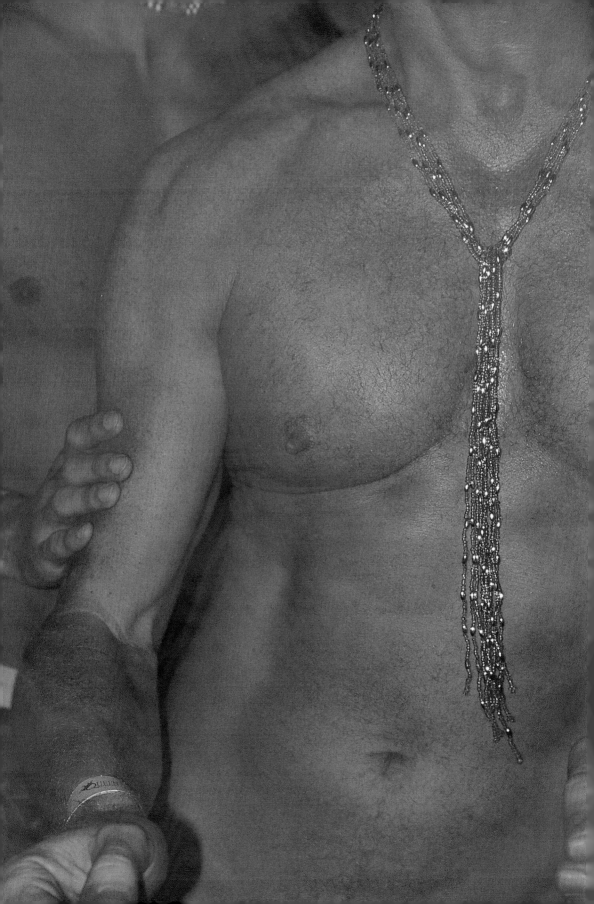

PARIS

"To know Paris is to know a great deal," said Henry

REVISITED

The city that might have seemed cold at first encounter becomes
welcoming, you start to know its streets and recognize its smells
and its sounds. Paris doesn't reveal its secrets lightly; but it
whispers them, and once you start to listen you feel like a
confidante. Its streets and its alleys, its tiny restaurants and
rarely opened doorways become your own. Memories heighten
the enjoyment, but there are always new discoveries to be made.

242

And when you've made the pilgrimage to gaze once again at the favourite painting, and lingered by the favourite fountain, what then? Paris should never be static. Wander instead into an unknown neighbourhood and see what happens. Become a Paris *flâneur*, throw away the *plan de Paris* and let your feet take you wherever they want to go. This is how to really discover the city.

Those who have time in Paris have the greatest luxury. Time to wander about the bookshops and the *quais*, to watch people go by over a long coffee or an apéritif, to sit and think. For all the frenetic bustle of its shops and boulevards, Paris was really made for doing nothing at all. Instead of always seeking out the same little space for a moment of quiet, why not discover one of the peripheral parks – the parc des Buttes Chaumont high up on its rock in the 20th arrondissement, or the Parc George Brassens in the 15th? Find a tiny church for contemplation rather than the vast edifice of Notre-Dame or St-Sulpice, or even venture out to the Bois de Boulogne, the Bois de Vincennes, the rocks of Fontainebleau and the forest of Marly.

Miller. That's the way Paris grows on you.

Paris also offers plenty of opportunities to delve deeper into French culture. Cooking schools, painting ateliers, auction houses and wine societies all run prestigious courses within which to immerse yourself in whatever milieu makes Paris special for you. Or, even better, take your own time to study wine and food by tasting in the various specialist food and wine shops, sketch in the galleries and visit the less well documented places that have inspired writers and painters – Bougival, where Renoir painted and Turgenev wrote, the architectural suburbs of Passy and Auteuil or present-day Montreuil, where instrument-makers, painters and dance studios have found their niche.

Paris doesn't have to be nostalgic – it can be a liberating city, where you explore new possibilities, take a walk (or a rollerblade) on the wild side. It can turn idle thought into fruitful ideas and ideas into possibilities. Make Paris, ordered, regimented, elaborately façaded Paris, your dreamscape and anything can happen. Above all, make Paris yours.

COURSES FOR CONNOISSEURS

If you want to dig deeper into French culture, learn to cook *à la française*, develop your palate for fine wines or gain more from Paris' museums and galleries there is an array of courses to choose from, that range from diplomas to lunchtime lectures.

Antiques

Even before the Paris salerooms became deregulated, allowing Christie's and Sotheby's to hold sales in the city, Christie's Education had an established programme of courses. As well as year-long diploma courses there are ten-week courses covering three periods from the Renaissance to the 20th century, evening courses in collecting photography and the new jurisdiction in the French art market, and lunchtime and evening lectures. There is a four-day course in English on the Art of Living in 18th century France, covering interior decoration, furniture, ceramics and fashion, ending with a gastronomic treat.

Art

The École du Louvre is a prestigious school in the Louvre itself, running art history and archaeology courses, while in the Carrousel du Louvre, the Union Central des Arts Décoratives has ateliers where you can study painting, sculpture, ceramics, life drawing and *trompe l'oeil*. The Paris Decorative and Fine Arts Society offers a series of lectures in English covering the major exhibitions and general fine arts.

An exciting and innovative course is to be found at the American University in Paris. "Art in Action: Creating Contemporary Art" offers evening sessions in the spring taught by painter and video artist Susan Shup. Visit contemporary art exhibitions, learn the theory behind art movements and push the limits of your imagination, drawing and sketching, even experimenting with video and sound. The AUP also runs an excellent summer course, "Photographing Paris", where you can learn the art of black-and-white photography in the style of Doisneau.

Cuisine

In the Ritz, the prestigious Ritz Escoffier École de Gastronomie Française expounds its modern approach to cooking. You can do just about anything here, from bread-making to a taking a professional diploma, and courses are available with simultaneous English translation. The other internationally recognized school is, of course, Le Cordon Bleu. Mirrors and video monitors and simultaneous translation allow you to follow the chef's every move at half-day demonstrations, week-long themed courses and diploma courses.

Alain Ducasse has opened his own cookery school at Argenteuil, led by the former Chef de Partie at the Plaza Athénée, Philippe Duc. Participants are kitted out in chef's uniforms and learn exactly what it is like to be part of a top restaurant's kitchen.

There is a lot of fun to be had, with a food and wine tasting at lunch. There are 12 ateliers, from Méditerranean, Povençal and multi-ethnic cuisine to those that concentrate on entrées, fish or chocolate.

For a more intimate approach, Françoise Meunier runs three-hour classes for amateur cooks preparing a complete three-course meal which is then tasted with a glass of wine in hand. Paule Caillat begins her courses at Promenades Gourmandes with a trip to the local market to buy the ingredients. Students then don aprons and prepare a three-course meal together.

French Language & Culture

Combining a course on French civilization and culture with learning the language can add an extra dimension to a stay in Paris. The British Insitute, held in high regard for its French and English language courses, also runs courses for adults in contemporary French culture and society, while its French counterpart, the Alliance Française, runs French courses and lectures on culture. The Institut Catholique also offers good, traditional courses in French language and culture and is not exclusive to Catholic students.

The Institut Parisien, a dynamic private school, offers courses in the language, civilization and also business French.Or, if you want to study at the queen of French universities, La Sorbonne has a *Cours de Langue et Civilisation*. Traditional grammar-based teaching incorporates lectures on French art, literature and history.

The American University in Paris runs two intensive three-week summer courses where students practice the language in real life situations such as restaurants and markets, with trips to museums, theatre and cinema too. What more enjoyable way to brush up on your French?

Wine

If you have a passion for wine you are in the right place. The CIDD (Centre d'Information, de Documentation et de Dégustation) is one of the best known wine societies. Professional training is complemented by conferences, themed weekends and tasting trips to vineyards, and some courses are available in French, English and Japanese. The Centre de Dégustation Jacques Vivet runs introductory and *perfectionnement* courses. While there is a lot of theory involved, Vivet claims to avoid wine snobbery. Some advance knowledge of wine is required at Grains Nobles, where you will be taken down to the cellar by founder André Bessou to taste some of France's finest wines. There are *dégustations* concentrating on a different wine each time, and *études de terroirs*, which are followed by a meal. The Institut du Vin du Savour Club, headed by former Ritz and Grand Véfour *sommelier* Georges Lepré, focuses on how to match wines to dishes. If your taste for finer things in life includes music, you'll enjoy the original approach at L'École du Vin Ylan Schwartz. Working with a baroque ensemble and musicians from the Orchestre Philharmonique de Radio France, Schwartz plans evenings that combine dinner, wine-tasting and the music to suit. There are also courses matching wine with foods and some are available in English or Spanish.

One of the most abiding images of Paris is of the *bouquinistes* along the *quais* of the Left Bank. The little lockable cabinets, weatherbeaten by years of wind, rain and sunshine, are an unchanging fixture along the Seine and even their wares seem to stay the same over the years – dog-eared copies of novels and *romans policiers*, the same old covers of *Paris Match* magazines featuring Bardot on the beach and Sophia Loren in her prime. In the '30s Hemingway used to go to a book stall near the Tour d'Argent where English language books left behind by foreigners in the restaurant's guest rooms were sold two a penny by a bookseller who considered them worthless if they weren't well illustrated and bound. Even then, the *bouqinistes* had been there for centuries – they are in fact one of the oldest trades in Paris.

BOOKLOVERS' PARIS

For a booklover there is no more delightful way to spend an afternoon in Paris than to trawl round the Latin Quarter's dusty bookshops. The foray must always start on the *quais* before crossing the road to Paris' most celebrated Anglophone bookshop, Shakespeare and Co. It is no longer run by Sylvia Beach, the publisher who acted as mentor to Hemingway, Joyce and a host of others, but Georges Whitman (and now his daughter, Sylvia) has given it a new kind of celebrity with his own method of encouraging young foreign writers – letting them stay in the rooms above the bookshop in exchange for working there while they find their feet in Paris. The rooms are crammed with books, chairs and sofas where you can browse, read and chat late into the night.

Another delightfully ramshackle bookshop is La Librairie du Pont Traversé, where art books are piled up next to the quintessential French cream-bound paperbacks (no pictures allowed) and antique leather-bound volumes. In fact, rue de Vaugirard is the booklovers' paradise in Paris, where, in summer, one shop after another spills its contents out onto the street. Some are high-brow antiquarian booksellers, others cater for art lovers and those who are looking for a little bit of Paris to take home in the form of photographs or poetry. La Hune, not far away on the boulevard St-Germain, has become a Left Bank institution, not only for its excellent selection of art books, French literature and criticism, but as a meeting place for young intellectuals – love has even been known to blossom among the bookshelves. As you move nearer to the Panthéon, the neoclassical resting place of France's "great men", the bookshops reflect a suitably sober tone. Here are the specialist booksellers for graduates in any discipline: one, devoted to philosophy, has a window display consisting entirely of plain cream volumes emblazoned with the name KANT. Clearly, plain speaking is a virtue that philosophers appreciate.

But philosophy, bookishness and pleasure need not be mutually exclusive. In the Marais district Hortense offers the ambrosial combination of a literary wine shop. The conversation at the bar of this cosy establishment can just as easily turn to *millésimé* as to Marxism as you sip a glass of your favourite Côtes du Rhône and turn the pages of books for sale that line the walls. Another very civilized bar that offers intellectual as well as liquid sustenance is the Fumoir, not far from the Louvre. The cocktail bar and restaurant are often filled with young professionals networking, but should you come here alone there is a library of 3,000 volumes to choose from. Only in Paris...

As for places to read, there are a wealth of libraries open to the public, from the glass towers of the Bibliothèque nationale de France François Mitterrand, centrepiece of the 13th arrondissement, to the Bibliothèque Historique de la Ville de Paris, housed in a beautiful Marais *hôtel particulier*, the Hôtel de Lamoignon. It has been a library since 1751, when the King's State Prosecutor built up a collection on the history of Paris and bequeathed it to the City. Maps, atlases, old photographs and manuscripts can be seen as well as literary collections. The Bibliothèque Mazarine in the Institut de France has a stunning reading room filled with antiques, busts and chandeliers that once belonged to the Cardinal himself, and can be used by anyone, providing there is room (there are only 140 seats).

But on a summer's day it is hard to resist the urge to be outside. Take your favourite book instead to the Jardin du Luxembourg and sit on one of the green-painted chairs under a lilac tree in the changing light. Few Paris pleasures can quite compare to this.

Despite its compactness, despite the regimentation of its arrondissements and the efficiency of its public transport system, there is still a hidden Paris, a Paris that evokes the photographs of Jean Atget and Brassaï and the films of Jean Renoir.

UNSUNG NEIGHBOURHOODS

Sometimes you can stray off the beaten track and suddenly find yourself in a world of cobbled streets and decaying buildings, where tiny shopfronts display arcane merchandise such as *hanukkah* candles or religious texts, while in a nearby café men huddle round card tables looking like gamblers from a *film noir*. The particular street evoked here, steeply climbing, its cobbles awash with rainwater, links the busy boulevard de Belleville to the modern Parc de Belleville, a little tract of time left behind by the developers. This *quartier*, with its mysteries and curiosities, its juxtapositions of old and new, ethnic and *vieille* Paris, is endlessly fascinating for the *flâneur*. Not far away, in the south-east corner of the 10th arrondissement, is another little enclave around the rue Ste-Marthe. Here, on a summer's evening as you sit at the tables in front of Le Panier café listening to neighbours calling to each other across the balconies, you feel as though you should be in southern Italy, not Paris.

The appeal of the 20th arrondissement is not lost on its residents, who relish the fact that being the last gives a false impression of somehow being miles from central Paris. Some intrepid tourists venture out to Père Lachaise and even to the Buttes-Chaumont park, which, with its hills, grottoes and vertiginous bridges, is well worth the trip, but rarely elsewhere. Yet just wandering the streets can lead you into lost worlds, such as that of the lovely Cité Hermitage, a cul-de-sac of artists' studios where tiny gardens that are the domain of myriad cats back onto a cobbled path lit by London-style street lamps. One of the best ways to discover the 20th is during the *portes ouvertes*, the open doors of artists' studios that takes place in September – less for the art perhaps than for the chance to wander in and out of places such as these, up dark staircases and into little rooms which look onto sprawling, verdant gardens. At last you see behind the mysterious gate of the Miroitterie, which is not a mosaic shop as its broken mirror tiles suggest but an artists' squat where a bizarre, comical moving sculpture made from old bicycle bits and pan lids makes a terrible racket. Young artists sit round on old brasserie *banquettes*, DJs spin records and a man paints spirals of butterflies that make you feel light-headed.

Another fascinating area for *flânerie* is the Batignolles, on the borders of Montmartre to the west of the place de Clichy. Though only streets away from the nightclubs of Pigalle, the area is quietly bohemian, its narrow streets lined with picture-framers and ethnic giftshops in between the workaday shoe shops and key cutters. It has a wonderful small hotel, the Eldorado, where the owner, Maria Gratacos, has filled the pension-like rooms with velvets, animal prints and *brocante* finds, and not-yet-famous models and writers sit in the plant-filled courtyard drinking glasses of *rosé*. A little bit further down the rue des Dames is the extraordinary *robinetterie* Salles de Bains Rétro where, defying minimalism, Nicolas has amassed a collection of antique bathroomware. Marble baths, taps in the shape of swans and crystal atomizers evoke a Belle Époque beauty's boudoir while in the workshop next door, amid a mish-mash of old accordions and Tiffany lights craftsmen restore Heath-Robinson showers and English rose-painted porcelain. Walk up the rue des Batignolles to the Square des Batignolles, a pretty garden with a bandstand and lake surrounded by antique shops with names like La Vie en Rose. In the weeks before Christmas in the church you may stumble on a nativity play acted out with moving simplicity by adults.

Quietly slumbering, tucked in beneath the Seine, the residential 15th arrondissement is the butt of many jokes about how nothing ever happens there. But there are things to be discovered – La Ruche, for instance, the curious "beehive" built by Eiffel for the 1900 Exhibition and moved here to become artists' studios, housing in its time such luminaries as Chagall, Modigliani and Zadkine. Starchly old-fashioned, the 15th also has the strikingly modern Parc André-Citroën, on the site of the old car factory, as well as the Parc Georges-Brassens, with its own vineyard.

The art of *flânerie* is really to not know where you are going, just to wander. It is one of Paris' great pleasures; so be liberated from the tyranny of the guidebook, at least for a day.

"WHEN PARIS HONOUR OF AD

YOU MUST BE AT HER DEVOTED TO

LOVING PARIS

FOR IT BECOMES SO NEC

BEGIN TO BEL

WE MAY BE OF

HAS DONE YOU THE

MITTING YOU,

BECK AND CALL,

HER EVERY WHIM.

MAKES US PROUD,

CESSARY THAT WE

IEVE THAT

SOME USE TO HER." SACHA GUITRY

Who would have thought that the rooftops of the Paris opera house contain more than 500 lovers' names carved into the lead? They are the mementos of dancers (whose rehearsal studio was right below), musicians, scene shifters, carpenters, doormen, and the Polytechnic students who used to have their ball in the Garnier building, all of whom climbed onto the roofs for a tender moment, looking down on sparkling Paris below.

PARIS FOR LOVERS

"A real library of love," is how Jean Mussau, retired scene shifter, describes the rooftop's secret stash of memories. Romantic Paris is not just the stuff of postcards, the iconic images of Doisneau's *Kiss* in front of the Hôtel de Ville or Willy Ronis' '50s couple embracing by the Pont-Royal. It is in the stories and dreams of its inhabitants, and all those who have visited and left with a heart filled with joy or sorrow. For love is never static in Paris. The strange alchemy of its changing light can turn friendship into passion, or reveal the flaws between two people who might have continued muddling through if not confronted by such splendour. Perhaps that's why an affair is an *histoire*, a story played out against a glorious backdrop. Wandering around the city one cannot help but invent stories around the characters one sees, their lives refracted through glass: glimpsed through the window of a café in passage Jouffroy, the intellectual, rather bohemian couple whose twirling cigarette smoke leaves question marks in the air; the middle-aged couple, perhaps reliving a wonderful spring afternoon 25 years ago as they walk hand in hand through the Latin Quarter; the two single people sensitively placed next to each other by the waiter at Maxim's – will they find the courage to strike up a conversation?

Still, as if planted by an unseen photographer, there are lovers everywhere, seemingly oblivious to the picture perfect image they create. Walking across the Pont Neuf that connects the Île de la Cité to the Left Bank you often see them, down on the *quai*, tenderly embracing. In the Tuilerie gardens romance blossoms in time with the lilac, and the café terraces on the place St-Sulpice are the scene for tentative first steps over an espresso and a discussion of Descartes. Did Doisneau start it all, or did he simply capture the romantic spirit of the city?

"WE WOULD GO, YOU AND I, WITH THAT ECSTATIC AIR THAT CHARACTERISES LOVERS IN SEARCH OF THINGS LIKE UNTO THEMSELVES, TO CONTEMPLATE, IN THE GALLERIE SULLY, GEORGE DE LA TOUR'S 'MADELEINE À LA VEILLEUSE'."

LINDA LÊ, 'TO SHE WHO IS ABSENT'

Paris for lovers is the Paris of parks and of water. The Canal St-Martin is a favourite lovers' walk, past the dreamy reflective water, in autumn filled with falling leaves, stopping for coffee or lunch at Chez Prune. Or the Jardin du Luxembourg, where the Medici fountain seems to have an irrepressible effect on couples who embrace even among the hordes of children throwing sticks into the water. Bridges, like the Pont Neuf with its little half-circle alcoves, are made for kissing, and the quais for lingering walks hand in hand.

There are restaurants made for romance, like the Pré Catalan in the Bois de Boulogne or Le Chalet des Îles, reached by boat across a lake. But even the simplest bistro with checked table-cloths can provide the food of love in the right company; your own, special place to be revisited on each trip back to Paris.

The writer Thom Elkjer claims that Parisians love not like other people, but in an Aristotelian way, made up of a series of carefully constucted debates. "Baron Haussmann's broad boulevards and great monuments argue eloquently that Paris is not like other cities, and its inhabitants not like other city dwellers," he says. "Why then should they love like others, with more feeling than reason?" It is true that a love affair in Paris can take involve hours of soul-searching over the coffee cups; it is all part of the ritual. But thankfully there is spontaneity too: how else could the ubiquitous rose sellers ever make a living?

The romance of Paris is not overwhelming, like that of Rome or Venice, but it is a city that makes you want to be in love. And in the end, whatever, or whoever, brought you here in the first place, Paris itself becomes the lover, whom you miss when you are absent, and who greets you when you return with familiar caresses and new delights. With poetry and light and movement – always difficult, always unpredictable, and quite impossible to leave.

One of the most uplifting views in Paris is from Belleville, as one exits from the Métro at Pyrénées. Here you are in one of the most defiantly working-class districts, where Edith Piaf once walked the streets singing for crumbs; yet look down and you see all Paris spread below and the Eiffel Tower, symbol of nothing other than that in Paris everything can be romantic.

שלום

vrede

béke

和平

和平

мир

ειρήνη

paz

صلح

vrieden fr

DIRECTORY

ONE: ARCHITECTURE

CHURCHES

Basilique du Sacré-Coeur
35 rue du Chevalier-de-la-
Barre, 18th
Tel: 01.53.41.89.00

Cathédrale Alexander
Nevsky
12 rue Daru, 8th
Tel: 01.42.27.37.34

Cathédrale Notre-Dame
de Paris
6 pl Parvis Notre-Dame, 4th
Tel: 01.44.32.16.70

Dome des Invalides
Hôtel National des Invalides,
129 rue Grenelle, 7th
Tel: 01.44.42.37.72

Eglise de la Madeleine
pl. de la Madeleine, 8th
Tel: 01.44.51.69.00

Eglise St-Ephrem-le-Syriaque
17 rue des Carmes
Musique et Patrimoine:
Tel: 01.42.50.96.18

Eglise St-Etienne du Mont
pl Ste-Geneviève, 5th
Tel: 01.43.54.11.79

Eglise St-Eugène
4 rue du Conservatoire, 9th
Tel: 01.48.24.70.25

Eglise St-Germain
l'Auxerrois
2 pl du Louvre, 1st
Tel: 01.42.60.13.96

Eglise St-Germain-des-Prés
3 pl St-Germain-des-Prés,
6th
Tel: 01.43.25.41.71

Eglise St-Julien-le-Pauvre
rue St-Julien-le-Pauvre, 5th
Tel: 01.43.54.52.16

Eglise St-Séverin
1 rue des Prêtres-St-
Séverin, 5th
Tel: 01.42.34.93.50

Eglise St-Sulpice
pl St-Sulpice, 6th
Tel: 01.46.33.21.78

La Sainte-Chapelle
4 bd du Palais, 1st
Tel: 01.53.73.78.50

MARAIS MANSIONS

Finkelsztajn
27 rue des Rosiers, 4th
Tel: 01.42.72.78.91

Musée d'Art et d'Histoire
du Judaïsme
Hôtel de St-Aignan,
71 rue du Temple, 3rd
Tel: 01.53.01.86.53
www.mahj.org

Musée Carnavalet
23 rue de Sévigné, 3rd
Tel: 01.44.59.58.58
www.paris-
france.org/musees

Musée National Picasso
Hôtel Salé, 5 rue de
Thorigny, 3rd
Tel: 01.42.71.25.21

Patrimoine Photographique
Hôtel de Sully, 62 rue St-
Antoine, 4th
Tel: 01.42.74.47.75
www.patrimoine-photo.org

Pavillon de la Reine
28 pl des Vosges, 3rd
Tel: 01.40.29.19.19
www.pavillon-de-la-
reine.com

REVOLUTION AND
REBIRTH

Musée Jacquemart-André
158 bd Haussmann, 8th
Tel: 01.42.89.04.91
www.musee-jacquemart-
andre.com

La Tour Eiffel
Champ de Mars, 7th
Tel: 01.44.11.23.45
Recorded information:
01.44.11.23.23
www.tour-eiffel.fr

Eiffel buildings:
Barrio Latino
46 rue du Fbg.St-Antoine,
12th
Tel: 01.55.78.84.75

Le Bon Marché
24 rue de Sèvres, 7th
Tel: 01.44.39.80.00
www.bonmarche.fr

La Ruche (artists' studios)
passage de Dantzig, 15th

MODERN PARIS
Cappellini
4 rue des Rosiers, 4th
Tel: 01.42.78.39.39

Castel Béranger
14 rue La Fontaine, 16th
(Closed to public)

Centre Pompidou
rue Beaubourg, 4th
Tel: 01.44.78.12.33

Cité de la Musique
221 av Jean-Jaurès, 19th
Tel: 01.44.84.44.84
www.cite-musique.fr

La Cité Universitaire
bd Jourdan, 14th
www.ciup.fr

Le Dôme
108 bd du Montparnasse,
14th
Tel: 01.43.35.25.81

Fondation Cartier pour
l'art contemporain
261 bd Raspail, 14th
Tel: 01.42.18.56.72
Recorded info:
01.42.18.56.51
www.fondation.cartier.fr

Fondation Le Corbusier
Villa La Roche, 10 square du
Dr-Blanche, 16th
Tel: 01.42.88.41.53
www.fondationle
corbusier.asso.fr

Insitut du Monde Arabe
1 rue des Fossés-St-Bernard,
5th
Tel: 01.40.51.38.38
www.imarabe.org

Kartell Flagship Shop
242 bd St Germain, 7th
Tel: 01.45.48.68.37

Lucas Carton
9 pl de la Madeleine, 8th
Tel: 01.42.65.22.90
www.lucascarton.com

Maison Prunier
16 av Victor Hugo, 16th
Tel: 01.44.17.35.85
www.maisonprunier.com

Musée d'Art Moderne de la
Ville de Paris
11 av du Président-Wilson,
16th
Tel: 01.53.67.40.00

Musée National d'Orsay
1 rue de la Légion
d'Honneur, 7th
Tel: 01.40.49.48.14
Recorded information:
01.45.49.11.11

Musée de la Publicité
Palais du Louvre, 107 rue
de Rivoli, 1st
Tel: 01.44.55.57.50
www.ucad.fr

Palais de Chaillot
pl du Trocadéro, 16th
Theatre:
Tel: 01.53.65.30.00
www.theatre-chaillot.fr

Palais de Tokyo: Site de
Création Contemporaine
13 av du Président-Wilson,
16th
Tel: 01.47.23.54.01
www.palaisdetokyo.com

Sentou Galerie
24 rue Pont Louis Philippe,
4th
Tel: 01.42.71.00.01;
26 bd Raspail, 7th
Tel: 01.45.49.00.05

Villa Savoye
82 rue de Villiers,
78300 Poissy
Tel: 01.39.65.01.06
www.fondationle
corbusier.asso.fr

TWO: CULTURE

INTRODUCTION

Comédie Française
Salle Richelieu pl Colette,
1st
Tel: 01.44.58.15.15
www.comedie-francaise.fr

Théâtre du Vieux-Colombier
21 rue du Vieux-Colombier,
6th
Tel: 01.44.39.87.00
www.comedie-francaise.fr

La Flèche d'Or
102 bis rue de Bagnolet,
20th
Tel: 01.43.72.42.44
www.flechedor.com

La Maison de Radio France
116 av du Président-
Kennedy, 16th
Tel: 01.42.30.22.22
Concert information:
01.42.30.15.16
www.radiofrance.fr

La Maroquinerie
23 rue Boyer, 20th
Tel: 01.40.33.30.60

Musée Marmottan –
Claude Monet
2 rue Louis-Boilly, 16th
Tel: 01.42.24.07.02
www.marmottan.com

Musée de la Mode et
du Textile
Palais du Louvre, 107 rue de
Rivoli, 1st
Tel: 01.44.55.57.50
www.ucad.fr

Musée National des Arts
Asiatiques – Guimet
6 pl d'Iéna, 16th
Tel: 01.56.52.53.00
www.museeguimet.fr

Musée National d'Orsay
1 rue de la Légion
d'Honneur, 7th
Tel: 01.40.49.48.14

Musée de l'Orangerie
Jardin des Tuileries, 1st
Tel: 01.42.97.48.16

L'Olympia
28 bd des Capucines, 9th
Reservations:
01.74.42.25.49
www.olympiahall.com

Opéra Comique
pl Boïeldieu, 2nd
Tel: 01.42.44.45.46
www.opera-comique.fr

Orangerie de la Bagatelle
Bois de Boulogne:
Festival Chopin
(mid-June to mid-July)
Tel: 01.45.00.22.19
www.frederic-chopin.com

Palais Omnisports de
Paris-Bercy
8 bd de Bercy, 12th
Tel: 08.03.03.00.31
www.bercy.fr

Salle Cortot
78 rue Cardinet, 17th
Tel: 01.47.63.85.72

Salle Pleyel
253 rue du Fbg-St-Honoré,
8th
Tel: 01.45.61.53.01
www.salle-pleyel.fr

Zénith
211 av Jean-Jaurès, 19th
Tel: 01.42.08.60.00
www.le-zenith.com

A NIGHT AT THE OPERA

L'Entracte
1 rue Auber, 9th
Tel: 01.47.42.26.25

Opéra Bastille
pl de la Bastille, 12th
Box office: 08.36.69.78.68
Guided tours:
01.40.01.19.70
www.opera-de-paris.fr

Palais Garnier
pl de l'Opéra, 9th
Box office: 08.36.69.78.68
Guided tours:
01.40.01.22.63
Museum: 01.40.01.24.93
www.opera-de-paris.fr

EXPLORING THE LOUVRE

Café Marly
93 rue de Rivoli, cour
Napoléon du Louvre, 1st
Tel: 01.49.26.06.60

Jeu de Paume
1 pl de la Concorde, 8th
Tel: 01.47.03.12.50

The Louvre
Entrance through Pyramid,
Cour Napoléon, 1st
Tel: 01.40.20.50.50
Recorded information:
01.40.20.51.51
www.louvre.fr

CINEMA

Action Ecoles
23 rue des Ecoles, 5th
Tel: 01.43.29.79.89

L'Atelier
95 rue Lemercier, 17th
Tel: 01.42.26.05.89

Café des Deux Moulins
15 rue Lepic, 18th

Au Casque d'Or
51 rue des Cascades, 20th
Tel: 01.43.58.44.55

Forum des Images
2 Grande Galerie, Porte
St-Eustache, Forum des
Halles, 1st
Tel: 01.44.76.62.00
www.forumdesimages.net

Le Grand Rex
1 bd Poissonnière, 2nd
Tel: 08.36.68.70.23
www.legrandrex.com

Hôtel du Nord
102 quai de Jemmapes,
10th
Tel: 01.53.19.98.88
www.anythingmatters.com

Hôtel du Septième Art
20 rue St-Paul, 4th
Tel: 01.44.54.85.00

La Pagode
57 bis rue de Babylone, 7th
Tel: 01.45.55.48.48

Parc de la Villette
au Corentin-Cariou, 19th
www.villette.com

Reflet Médicis Logos
5 rue Champollion, 5th
Tel: 01.43.54.26.42

Studio 28
10 rue Tholozé, 18th
Tel: 01.46.06.36.07

SMALL MUSEUMS

Atelier-Musée Henri
Bouchard
25 rue de l'Yvette, 16th
Tel: 01.46.47.63.46
www.musee-bouchard.com

Musée du Cristal Baccarat
30 bis rue de Paradis, 10th
Tel: 01.47.70.64.30
www.baccarat.fr

Musée Edith Piaf
5 rue Crespin-du-Gast, 11th
Tel: 01.43.55.52.72

Musée de l'Eventail
2 bd de Strasbourg, 10th
Tel: 01.42.08.90.20

Musée Gustav Moreau
14 rue de La
Rochefoucauld, 9th
Tel: 01.48.74.38.50

Musée Nissim de Camondo
63 rue de Monceau, 8th
Tel: 01.53.89.06.40
www.ucad.fr

Musée de la Vie
Romantique
16 rue Chaptal, 9th
Tel: 01.48.74.95.38

Musée Zadkine
100 bis rue d'Assas, 6th
Tel: 01.43.26.91.90

PARIS AND THE
AVANT-GARDE

Centre Mandapa
6 rue Wurtz, 13th
Tel: 01.45.89.01.60

Centre Momboye
25 rue Boyer, 20th
Tel: 01.43.58.85.01
www.ladanse.com/
momboye

Chez Robert-Electron Libre
59 rue de Rivoli, 1st
www.59rivoli.org
(open for art viewing
1.30-7.30pm Mon-Sat)

Cité de la Musique
(see under ARCHITECTURE;
Modern Paris)

L'Etoile du Nord
16 rue Georgette-Agutte,
18th
Tel: 01.42.26.47.47

Festival d'automne
www.festival-automne.com

Institut du Monde Arabe
(see under ARCHITECTURE;
Modern Paris)

Iranian Cultural Centre
(Centre Cultural Pouya)
48 bis quai de Jemmapes,
10th
Tel: 01.42.08.38.47
www.pouya.org

IRCAM
1 pl Igor-Stravinsky, 4th
Tel: 01.44.78.48.16
www.ircam.fr

Palais de Tokyo: Site de
Création Contemporaine
(see under ARCHITECTURE;
Modern Paris)

Le Regard du Cygne
210 rue de Belleville, 20th
Tel: 01.43.58.55.93
http://redcygne.free.fr

Studio CND
15 rue Geoffroy-l'Asnier,
4th
Tel: 01.42.74.06.44

Théâtre de la Bastille
76 rue de la Roquette,
11th
Tel: 01.43.57.42.14

Théâtre des Champs-Elysées
15 av Montaigne, 8th
Tel: 01.49.52.50.50
www.theatrechamps
elysees.fr

Théâtre de la Ville
2 pl du Châtelet, 4th
Tel: 01.42.74.22.77
www.theatredelaville-
paris.com

THREE: RETAIL
PLEASURES

THE GREAT AGE
OF SHOPPING

BHV (Bazar de l'Hôtel
de Ville)
52-64 rue de Rivoli, 4th
Tel: 01.42.74.90.00
www.bhv.fr

Castelbajac Concept Store
31 pl du Marché-St-Honoré,
1st
Tel: 01.42.60.41.55

Colette
213 rue St-Honoré, 1st
Tel: 01.55.35.33.90
www.colette.fr

Le Bon Marché
24 rue de Sèvres, 7th
Tel: 01.44.39.80.00
www.bonmarche.fr

Galeries Lafayette
40 bd Haussmann, 9th
Tel: 01.42.82.34.56
www.galerieslafayette.com
Cigar cellar: 99 rue
de Provence

Printemps
64 bd Haussmann, 9th
Tel: 01.42.82.50.00
www.printemps.com

La Samaritaine
19 rue de la Monnaie, 1st
Tel: 01.40.41.20.20
www.lasamaritaine.com

Spree
16 rue de La Vieuville, 18th
Tel: 01.42.23.41.40

LES BONNES ADRESSES

Alice Cadolle
14 rue Cambon, 1st
Tel: 01.42.60.94.94

A l'Imagerie
9, rue Dante, 5th
Tel: 01.43.25.18.66
www.alimagerie.com

Amin Kader
2 rue Guisarde, 6th
Tel: 01.43.26.27.37

Arôm
73 av Ledru-Rollin, 12th
Tel: 01.43.46.82.59

Le Cachemirien
13 rue du Tournon, 6th
Tel: 01.43.29.93.82

Calligrane
4-6 rue du Pont Louis-
Philippe, 4th
Tel: 01.48.04.31.89

Caravane
6 rue Pavée, 4th
Tel: 01.44.61.04.20
www.caravane.fr

Caravane Chambre 19
19 rue St Nicolas, 12th
Tel: 01.53.02.96.96

Catherine Memmi
11 rue St Sulpice, 6th
Tel: 01.44.07.02.02

Christian Tortu
6 carrefour de l'Odéon, 6th
Tel: 01.43.26.02.56

Comptoir des Ecritures
35 rue Quincampoix, 4th
Tel: 01.42.78.95.10

Dîners en Ville
27 rue de Varenne, 7th
Tel: 01.42.22.78.33

E. Dehillerin
8 rue Coquilliere, 1st
Tel: 01.42.36.53.13

Editions de Parfums
Frédéric Malle
37 rue de Grenelle, 7th
Tel: 01.42.22.77.22

Erès
2 rue Tronchet, 8th
Tel: 01.47.42.28.82

Fiesta Galerie
45 rue Vielle du Temple, 4th
Tel: 01.42.71.53.34

Irina Volkonski
45 rue Madame, 6th
Tel: 01.42.22.02.37

Lydia Courteille
33, rue Mazarine, 6th
231 rue St-Honoré, 8th

Naïla de Monbrison
6 rue de Bourgogne, 7th
Tel: 01.47.05.1.15

Orphée
8 rue du Pont Louis Philippe
Tel: 01.42.72.68.42

Parfums Caron
34 av Montaigne, 8th
Tel: 01.47.23.40.82

Paule Ka
20 rue Malher, 4th
Tel: 01.40.29.96.03

Severine Peraudin
5 place Saint Sulpice, 6th
Tel: 01.43.54.23.16

La Reine Margot
7 quai de Conti, 6th
Tel: 01.43.26.62.50

COVERED PASSAGEWAYS

l'Arbre à Cannelle
57 passage des Panoramas,
2nd
Tel: 01.45.08.55.87

Emilio Robba
29 galerie Vivienne, 2nd
Tel: 01.42.60.43.46

Galerie Vivienne
rue 6 Vivienne/4 rue des
Petits-Champs, 2nd

Hotel Chopin
46 passage Jouffroy, 9th
Tel: 01.47.70.58.10

Jousseaume
45 galerie Vivienne, 2nd
Tel: 01.42.96.06.24

Legrand Filles et Fils
1 rue de la Banque, 2nd
Tel: 01.42.60.07.12

Mercier, Graveur Imprimeur
8 passage des Panoramas,
2nd
Tel: 01.42.36.37.22

Nathalie Garçon
15 Galerie Vivienne, 2nd
Tel: 01.40.20.14.00

Pain d'épice
29 passage Jouffroy, 9th
Tel: 01.47.70.08.68

Passage Brady
rue du Fbg-St Denis/rue du
Fbg St-Martin, 10th

Passage Jouffroy
10-12 bd Montmartre/9 rue
de la Grange-Batelière, 9th

Passage des Panoramas
10 rue St-Marc/11 bd
Montmartre, 2nd

M.G.W. Segas
34 passage Jouffroy, 9th
Tel: 01.47.70.89.65

Stern, Graveur
47 passage des Panoramas,
2nd
Tel: 01.45.08.86.45

BROCANTES AND
THE PUCES

Christie's
9 av Matignon, 8th
Tel: 01.40.76.85.85

Drouot
9 rue Drouot, 9th
Tel: 01.48.00.20.20
www.drouot.fr

Louvre des Antiquaires
2 pl du Palais-Royal, 1st
Tel: 01.42.97.27.00
www.louvre-antiquaires.com

Ludlow
142 rue des Rosiers,
Marché Malassis, Marché
de Clignancourt;
15 rue des Beaux Arts, 6th
Tel: 01.43.29.06.44

Sotheby's
76 rue du Fbg St-Honoré,
8th
Tel: 01.53.05.53.05

THE SECRET ATELIERS
OF PARIS

Gérard Brucato
179 Fbg St-Antoine, 11th
Tel: 01.46.28.64.49

Michel Fey
Viaduc des Arts, 15 av
Daumesnil
Tel: 01.43.41.22.22

L. Laverdure & Fils
58 rue Traversière, 12th
Tel: 01.43.43.38.85

Le Promenade Plantée
av Daumesnil, 12th

Le Viaduc des Arts
15-121 av Daumesnil, 12th
www.viaduc-des-arts.com

FOUR: GASTRONOMIC PLEASURES

HAUTE CUISINE
See Paris' Best Restaurants, *below*

PARIS' BEST RESTAURANTS

Bon
25 rue de la Pompe, 16th
Tel: 01.40.72.70.00

Le Cinq
Hôtel Four Seasons George V
31 av George V, 8th
Tel: 01.49.52.70.00
www.fourseasons.com

Le Bristol
Hôtel Bristol
112 rue du Fbg-St-Honoré, 8th
Tel: 01.53.43.43.00
www.hotel-bristol.com

Guy Savoy
18 rue Troyon, 17th
Tel: 01.43.80.40.61
www.guysavoy.com

Hiramatsu
7 quai de Bourbon, 4th
Tel: 01.56.81.08.80

Alain Ducasse au Plaza Athénée
Hôtel Plaza Athénée
25 av Montaigne, 8th
Tel: 01.53.67.65.00
www.alain-ducasse.com

Les Ambassadeurs
Hôtel de Crillon, 10 pl de la Concorde, 8th
Tel: 01.44.71.16.16
www.crillon.com

L'Arpège
84 rue de Varenne, 7th
Tel: 01.45.51.47.33
www.alain-passard.com

L'Astrance
4 rue Beethoven, 16th
Tel: 01.40.50.84.40

L'Espadon
Hôtel Ritz, 15 pl Vendôme, 1st
Tel: 01.43.16.30.80
www.ritzparis.com

L'Esplanade
52 rue Fabert, 7th
Tel: 01.47.05.38.80

Georges
Centre Pompidou, 6th floor, rue Rambuteau, 4th
Tel: 01.44.78.47.99

Le Grand Véfour
17 rue de Beaujolais, 1st
Tel: 01.42.96.56.27

Lucas Carton
9 pl de la Madeleine, 8th
Tel: 01.42.65.22.90
www.lucascarton.com

Maison Blanche
15 av Montaigne, 8th
Tel: 01.47.23.55.99

Market
15 av Matignon, 8th
Tel: 01.56.43.40.90

Pierre Gagnaire
6 rue Balzac, 8th
Tel: 01.58.36.12.50
www.pierre-gagnaire.com

Le Pré Catalan
route de Suresnes, Bois de Boulogne, 16th
Tel: 01.44.14.41.14
www.lenotre.fr

Spoon, Food & Wine
14 rue de Marignan, 8th
Tel: 01.40.76.34.44

Tanjia
23 rue de Ponthieu, 8th
Tel: 01.42.25.95.00

La Tour d'Argent
15-17 quai de la Tournelle, 5th
Tel: 01.43.54.23.31
www.tourdargent.com

BRASSERIES AND BISTROS

Au 35
35 rue Jacob, 6th
Tel: 01.42.60.23.24

L'Avant-Goût
26 rue Bobillot, 13th
Tel: 01.53.80.24.00

Brasserie Lipp
151 bd St-Germain, 6th
Tel: 01.45.48.53.91
www.brasserie-lipp.fr

Charlot, Roi des Coquillages
81 bd de Clichy, 9th
Tel: 01.53.20.48.00

Chez La Vieille
1 rue Bailleul/37 rue de
l'Arbre Sec, 1st
Tel: 01.42.60.15.78

Le Colimaçon
44 rue Vieille-du-Temple,
4th
Tel: 01.48.87.12.01
www.lecolimacon.com

La Coupole
102 bd du Montparnasse,
14th
Tel: 01.43.20.14.20

Le Dôme
108 bd Montparnasse, 14th
Tel: 01.43.35.25.81

L'Européen
2 rue de Lyon, 12th
Tel: 01.43.43.99.70

Le Square Trousseau
1 rue Antoine-Vollon, 12th
Tel: 01.43.43.06.00

La Table de Lucullus
129 rue Legendre, 17th
Tel: 01.40.25.02.68

Thoumieux
79 rue St-Dominique, 7th
Tel: 01.47.05.49.75

Le Train Bleu
Gare de Lyon, place Louis-
Armand, 12th
Tel: 01.43.43.09.06

A PERFECT FOOD DAY

Berthillon
31 rue St Louis en l'Ile, 4th
Tel: 01.43.54.31.61

Marie-Anne Cantin
12 rue du Champs-de-Mars,
7th
Tel: 01.45.50.43.94
www.cantin.fr

L'Epicerie de l'Ile St-Louis
51 rue St-Louis-en-l'Ile, 4th
Tel: 01.43.25.20.14

Fauchon
26-30 pl de la Madeleine, 8th
Tel: 01.47.42.60.11

La Grande Epicerie de Paris
38 rue de Sèvres, 7th
Tel: 01.44.39.81.00

Hédiard
21 pl de la Madeleine, 8th
Tel: 01.43.12.88.88
www.hediard.fr

Pierre Hermé
72 rue Bonaparte, 6th
Tel: 01.43.54.47.77

Les Jardins du Luxembourg
pl Auguste-Comte,
pl Edmond-Rostand *or*
rue de Vaugirard, 6th

Jean-Luc Poujauran
20 rue Jean-Nicot, 7th
Tel: 01.47.05.80.88

MARKETS

Bd Auguste-Blanqui, 13th
(mornings, Tue, Fri, Sun)

Bd Raspail, 14th
(mornings, Sun)

Bd Richard-Lenoir, 12th
(mornings, Thur and Sun)

Marché Aligre, 12th
(daily)

Place du Guignier, 20th
(mornings, Thur and Sun)

Rue Daguerre, 14th
(daily)

Rue Montorgueil, 1st
(daily)

Rue Mouffetard, 5th
(daily)

CAFE LIFE
Bar du Marché
75 rue de Seine, 6th
Tel: 01.43.26.55.15

Café Charbon
109 rue Oberkampf, 11th
Tel: 01.43.57.55.13
www.nouveaucasino.net

Café Les Deux Magots
6 pl St Germain des Prés,
6th
Tel: 01.45.48.55.25

Cafe de Flore
172 bd St Germain, 6th
Tel: 01.45.48.55.26

Café de la Paix
3 place de l'Opéra, 9th
Tel: 01.40.07.30.10

La Coquille
30 rue Coquillière, 1st
Tel: 01.40.26.55.36

La Maroquinerie
23 rue Boyer, 20th
Tel: 01.40.33.30.60

Au Petit Fer à Cheval
30 rue Vieille-du-Temple,
4th
Tel: 01.42.72.47.47
www.cafeine.com

Au Vieux Colombier
65 rue de Rennes, 6th
Tel: 01.45.48.53.81

Web Bar
32 rue de Picardie, 3th
Tel: 01.42.72.66.55

FIVE: SEASONAL HIGHLIGHTS

THE COLLECTIONS
Didier Ludot
19, 20 23, 24 galerie
Montpensier, 1st
Tel: 01.42.96.06.56
www.didierludot.com
Little black dress shop
125 galerie Valois, 1st
Tel: 01.40.15.01.04

SPORTING EVENTS
Hippodrome de Chantilly
Chantilly
Tel: 03.44.62.41.00

Hippodrome de Longchamp
Bois de Boulogne, 16th
Tel: 01.44.30.75.00

Hippodrome d'Auteuil
Bois de Boulogne, 16th
Tel: 01.40.71.47.47

Philippe Model
33 place du Marché St-
Honoré, 1st
Tel: 01.42.96.89.02

Tête en l'Air
65 rue des Abbesses, 18th
Tel: 01.46.06.71.19

THE CIRCUS
Cirque d'Hiver Bouglione
110 rue Amelot, 11th
Tel: 01.47.00.12.25
www.cirquedhiver.com

Cirque Joseph Bouglione
(various venues)
Tel: 01.45.00.59.28
www.bouglione.com

Cirque Pinder
37 rue de Coulagnes,
94370 Sucy en Brie
Tel: 01.45.90.21.25
www.cirquepinder.com

La Journée au Cirque
Cirque de Paris, 115 bd
Charles de Gaulle, 92390
Villeneuve la Garenne
Tel: 01.47.99.40.40

Espace Châpiteau
Parc de la Villette, 19th
Tel: 01.40.03.75.15
www.villette.com

Romanes Cirque Tsiganè
12 rue Paul-Bert, 11th
Tel: 01.40.09.24.20

THE FOODIE CALENDAR

Salon de l'Agriculture
end March, Paris-Expo,
Porte de Versailles, 15th
Tel: 01.49.09.60.00
www.salon-agriculture.com

Salon Paris Fermiers
mid-October, Espace
Champerret, place de la
Porte Champerret, 17th
Tel: 01.43.95.16.92

Salon des Vins des
Vignerons Indépendants
April, December, Paris-Expo,
Porte de Versailles, 15th
Tel: 01.43.95.37.00

Salon du Chocolat
early October, often in the
Carrousel du Louvre
Tel: 01.45.03.21.26

Salon du Champignon
mid-October, Jardin des
Plantes, 5th
Tel: 01.40.79.36.00
www.mnhn.fr

SIX: AFTER DARK

COCKTAILS AT THE RITZ

The Hemingway Bar at
The Ritz
15 place Vendôme, 1st
Tel: 01.43.16.33.65

JAZZ IN PARIS

L'Arbuci Jazz Club
25 rue Buci, 6th
Tel: 01.44.32.16.00

La Balle au Bond
55 quai de la Tournelle, 5th
Tel: 01.40.51.87.06
www.laballeaubond.fr

Le Baiser Salé
58 rue des Lombards, 1st
Tel: 01.42.33.37.71

Le Bilboquet
13 rue St-Benoît, 6th
Tel: 01.45.48.81.84

Les 7 Lézards
10 rue des Rosiers, 4th
Tel: 01.48.87.08.97

Caveau de la Huchette
5 rue de la Huchette, 5th
Tel: 01.43.26.65.05

Duc des Lombards
42 rue des Lombards, 1st
Tel: 01.42.33.22.88

Les Instants Chavirés
7 rue Richard Lenoir, 93100
Montreuil
Tel: 01.42.87.25.91

New Morning
7-9 rue des Pétites-Ecuries,
10th
Tel: 01.45.23.51.41

Péniche Blues Café
Quai de la Gare, 13th
Tel: 01.45.84.24.88

Petit Journal St Michel
71 bd St Michel, 5th
Tel: 01.43.26.28.59

Le Petit Opportun
15 rue des Lavandières-
Ste-Opportune, 1st
Tel: 01.42.36.01.36

Le Sunset/Le Sunside
60 rue des Lombards, 1st
Tel:
Sunset: 01.40.26.46.60
Sunside: 01.40.26.21.25

HOT SPOTS

Atelier Renault
53 av des Champs-Elysées,
8th
Tel: 01.49.53.70.00

Barfly
49 av George V, 8th
Tel: 01.53.67.84.60

Le Buddha Bar
8 rue Boissy d'Anglas, 8th
Tel: 01.53.05.90.00

Café Charbon
109 rue Oberkampf, 11th
Tel: 01.43.57.55.13

Cithéa
112 rue Oberkampf, 11th
Tel: 01.40.21.70.95

Hôtel Costes
239 rue St-Honoré, 1st
Tel: 01.42.44.50.25

Man Ray
34 rue Marbeuf, 8th
Tel: 01.56.88.36.36
www.manray.fr

Nirvana
3 av Matignon, 8th
Tel: 01.53.89.18.91

Le Reflet
14 rue Serpente, 6th
Tel: 01.40.46.02.72

Tanjia
23 rue de Ponthieu, 8th
Tel: 01.42.25.95.00

CABARET

Casino de Paris
16 rue de Clichy, 9th
Tel: 01.49.95.22.22

Le Chat Noir
68 bd Clichy, 18th
Tel: 01.46.06.94.28

Crazy Horse Saloon
12 av George V, 8th
Tel: 01.47.23.32.32

Elysée Montmartre
72 bd Rochechouart, 18th
Tel: 01.44.92.45.38

Folies-Bèrgère
8 rue Saulnier, 9th
Tel: 01.44.79.98.98

Au Lapin Agile
22 rue Saules, 18
Tel: 01.46.06.85.87

Le Lido
116 bis av des Champs-
Elysées, 8th
Tel: 01.40.76.56.10
www.lido.fr

Le Moulin Rouge
82 bd de Clichy, 18th
Tel: 01.53.09.82.82
www.moulin-rouge.com

La Nouvelle Eve
25 rue de la Fontaine, 9th
Tel: 01.48.78.37.96

Le Zèbre
63 bd de Belleville, 20th
Tel: 01.47.99.40.40

WHERE TO DANCE

Barrio Latino
46 rue du Fbg. St-Antoine,
12th
Tel: 01.55.78.84.75

La Casa del Tango
11 allée Darius Milhaud,
19th
Tel: 01.40.40.73.60

Chez Gégène
162 bis quai de Polangis,
94340 Joinville-le-Pont
Tel: 01.48.83.29.43

Chez Louisette
130, avenue Michelet
(Marché Vernaison),
93400 Saint Ouen
Tel: 01.40.12.10.14

Chez Raymonde
119 av Parmentier, 11th
Tel: 01.43.55.26.27

Dancing at La Coupole
102 bd Montparnasse, 14th
Tel: 01.43.27.56.00

Le Guinguette du
Martin-Pêcheur
41 quai Victor-Hugo, 94500
Champigny-sur-Marne
Tel: 01.49.83.03.02

La Java
105 rue du Fbg du Temple,
10th
Tel: 01.42.02.20.52

La Pachanga
8 rue Vandamme, 14th
Tel: 01.56.80.11.40

COURSES FOR CONNOISSEURS

Alliance Française
101 bd Raspail, 6th
Tel: 01.42.84.90.00

The American University
of Paris
Summer Programs Office
102 rue Saint Dominique, 5th
Tel: 01.40.62.06.14
www.aup.edu

British Insitute in Paris
11 rue de Constantine
75340 Paris
Tel: 01.44.11.73.73

Centre de Dégustation
Jacques Vivet
48 rue de Vaugirard, 6th
Tel: 01.43.25.96.30

Centre de Formation
Alain Ducasse
41 rue de l'Abbé Ruellan
95100 Argenteuil
Tel: 01.34.34.19.10
www.atelier-
gastronomique.com

Christie's Education
Hôtel Salomon de Rothschild
11 rue Berryer, 8th
Tel: 01.42.25.10.90

CIDD Découverte du Vin
30 rue de la Sablière, 14th
Tel: 01.45.45.44.20

Le Cordon Bleu
8 rue Léon-Delhomme, 15th
Tel: 01.53.68.22.50

Ecole du Louvre
Porte Jaugard, Aile de Flore,
Palais du Louvre, quai du
Louvre, 1st
Tel: 01.55.35.19.35

L'Ecole du Vin Ylan Schwartz
17 passage Foubert, 13th
Tel: 01.45.89.77.39

Françoise Meunier
7 rue Paul-Lelong, 2nd
Tel: 01.40.26.14.00

Grains Nobles
5 rue Laplace, 5th
Tel: 01.43.54.93.54

Institut Catholique de Paris
12 rue Cassette, 6th
Tel: 01.44.39.52.68
www.icp.fr

Institut Parisien de Langue
et de Civilisation Françaises
87 bd Grenelle, 15th
Tel: 01.40.56.09.53

Insitut du Vin du Savour Club
11-13 rue Gros, 16th
Tel: 01.42.30.94.18

Paris Decorative and Fine
Arts Society
29 bd Lannes, 16th
Tel: 01.45.03.16.19

Promendes Gourmandes
187 rue du Temple, 3rd
Tel: 01.48.04.56.84

Ritz Escoffier Ecole de
Gastonomie Française
38 rue Cambon, 1st
Tel: 01.43.16.30.50

La Sorbonne (Cours de
Langue et Civilisation)
47 rue des Ecoles, 5th
Tel: 01.40.46.22.11

Union Central des Arts
Décoratives (UCAD)
111 rue de Rivoli, 1st
Tel: 01.44.55.59.02

BOOKLOVERS' PARIS

La Belle Hortense
31 rue Vielle-du-Temple, 4th
Tel: 01.48.04.71.60

Bibliothèque Historique de
la Ville de Paris
Hôtel Lamoignon,
24 rue Pavée, 4th
Tel: 01.44.59.29.40

Bibliothèque Mazarine
58 rue de Richelieu, 2nd
Tel: 01.53.79.53.79
www.bnf.fr

Bibliothèque Nationale de
France François Mitterrand
quai François-Mauriac, 13th
Tel: 01.53.79.53.79
www.bnf.fr

Le Fumoir
6 rue de l'Amiral-de-
Coligny, 1st
Tel: 01.42.92.00.24
www.lefumoir.com

La Hune
170 bd St Germain, 6th
Tel: 01.45.48.35.85

La Librairie du Pont Traversé
62 rue du Vaugirard, 6th
Tel: 01.45.48.06.48

Shakespeare and Co
37 rue de la Bûcherie, 5th
Tel: 01.43.26.96.50

UNSUNG NEIGHBOURHOODS

Cimetière du Père Lachaise
Main entrance: bd de
Ménilmontant, 20th
Tel: 01.55.25.82.10

Hôtel Eldorado
18 rue des Dames, 17th
Tel: 01.45.22.35.21/fax:
01.43.87.25.97
www.elderado.cityvox.com

Le Panier
32 rue Ste Marthe, 10th
Tel: 01.42.01.38.18

Parc André Citroën
rue Balard, rue St-Charles,
quai Citroën, 15th

Parc des Buttes-Chaumont
rue Botzaris, rue Manin, rue
de Crimée, 19th

La Ruche
passage de Dantzig, 15th

Salles de Bains Rétro
29-31 rue des Dames, 17th
Tel: 01.43.87.88.00
www.sbrparis.com

PARIS FOR LOVERS

Le Chalet des Iles
av Henri Martin/rue de la
Pompe, lac du Bois de
Boulogne, 16th
Tel: 01.42.88.04.69

Chez Prune
71 quai de Valmy, 10th
Tel: 01.42.41.30.47

Jardins du Luxembourg
pl Auguste-Comte,
pl Edmond-Rostand *or*
rue de Vaugirard, 6th

Le Pré Catalan
(*see under* GASTRONOMIC
PLEASURES; Paris' Best
Restaurants)

INTRODUCTION

Evening light glints on the Paris rooftops, where satellite dishes hide between the chimneypots and 19th century friezes.

Haussmannian façades reflected in the bonnet of a Citroën DS as it glides through the 16th arrondissement.

Colonnades of the Palais-Royal, built in 1629 for Cardinal Richelieu, reflected in the 20th century silver ball fountain of Paul Bury.

Patterned tiles inset into walls of the Pagode cinema at 57bis, rue de Babylone, 7th. A reproduction of a Japanese pagoda, it was built by the director of the Bon Marché as a present for his wife and became a cinema in 1931.

A lone visitor contemplates the infinite at the Insitut du Monde Arabe, seen through one of the 1,600 window panels that comprise its walls. Inspired by the screens of Moorish palaces, they open and close like the iris of an eye according to natural light levels.

Sudden sunlight as visitors emerge from the Cour Carré of the Louvre in front of I.M. Pei's glass pyramid.

Galerie Vivienne, the smartest of Paris' 19th century covered passageways. Built to protect bourgeois gowns and slippers from the mud and rain of the Paris streets, the galeries introduced the art of window shopping and became a fashionable place to meet.

Newly cleaned, a decapitated saint holds his head high over the doors of the west front at Notre-Dame Cathedral.

Feline faces and a message of peace in the Jardin des Plantes.

Climbing the staircase in search of culture at the Louvre.

On the tip of the Île St-Louis, summer bodies soak up the sun.

A shady resting place in the Cimetière de Montmartre.

The Italianate Fontaine de Médicis in the Jardins du Luxembourg is a favourite lovers' trysting point, despite the anguished figure of the Cyclops.

Conceived as a church, the Panthéon, seen here from the Jardins du Luxembourg, became an embarrassment to Revolutionary leaders and was reconsecrated as a 'temple of reason and resting place of great men'.

The Colonne de la Grande Armée in Place Vendôme is modelled on Trajan's column in Rome and depicts Napoléon's military exploits.

Wheels of all kinds keep the Paris streets abuzz – even the police are equipped with rollerblades.

The Friday Night Roller Rally has become an institution. Attracting as many as 25,000 rollerbladers, it takes over the city streets for a thrilling three-hour ride starting at Montparnasse.

CHAPTER ONE

Jean Nouvel's striking Institut du Monde Arabe, commissioned by François Mitterrand as one of his *Grands Projets*, is one of Paris' liveliest cultural centres, incorporating a library, concert *salles*, tea salon and museum.

The Opéra Bastille, designed by the Canadian-Uruguayan Carlos Ott, may not been the most popular of Mitterrand's *Grands Projets* but has resulted in the rejuvenation of the Bastille area.

A strikingly modern chimney in the Beaugrenelle quarter of the 15th arrondissement.

Sunlight on a moulded stone column at Castel Béranger brings to mind the lightly toasted meringues seen in many pâtisserie windows.

One of Paris' most famous and glorious sights, the rose window at Notre-Dame cathedral.

The Roue de Paris, the Millennium's Big Wheel, seen from behind the Place de la Concorde obelisk.

Napoléonic folly: the Arc du Carrousel at the entrance to the Louvre was built by the Emperor to celebrate his victories and predates the Arc de Triomphe.

The Neoclassical grandeur of the Panthéon, designed by Germain Soufflot. The crypt containing the tombs of Voltaire, Rousseau and other greats, lies below the church-like dome.

The Baroque sunburst altarpiece of Eglise St-Roch on rue St-Honoré. On account of its wonderful acoustics the church is often the venue for concerts.

An atmosphere of calm pervades the new Eglise de Notre-Dame d'Espérance on rue de la Roquette in the 11th, designed by Bruno Legrand to replace a joyless Art Deco church.

The Pont de Bir-Hakeim, famed for its part in the Bertolucci film *Last Tango in Paris*.

Sacré-Coeur basilica is a ghostly vision at night as you speed by on line 2 of the Métro.

The Pyramid du Louvre in blue mood.

Topiary in the Jardin des Invalides during a rare Paris snowfall.

New and old are juxtaposed at the Marché St-Honoré, a glass and metal structure by Ricardo Bofill that echoes the glass pavilions by Baltard that once stood there. It houses the Paribas bank.

Kaleidoscopic play of light at the Institut du Monde Arabe.

Parisian letterboxes, in the hallways to shared apartment buildings, are one of the distinctive features of life in the city. Now that concierges are a rarity, postmen have to remember the security door codes for every building.

These melancholy and mysterious figures can be found half-submerged in a wall beside Père Lachaise cemetery.

Peeling paint adds charm to a courtyard doorway off the 11th arrondissement's rue Saint-Sabin.

A stuccoed double doorway on rue Etienne Marcel in the 3rd arrondissement demands a more rigorous method of entry.

Balconies – an all-important window on the world for apartment dwellers – take many forms, from the bucolic, trailing plants and washing lines of north and east Paris to smart minimalism and the decorative excesses of the Haussmann and Art Nouveau eras.

The Medieval Hotel de Sens, one of the Marais' most distinctive *hôtels particuliers*, was built as a *pied à terre* for the bishops of Sens and is now home to the Bibliothèque Forney library of decorative arts.

Gustave Caillebot's *Man on a Balcony*, c.1880.

Encrusted with ornate decoration, Third Empire balconies line a tree-filled boulevard.

Maximilien Luce's *Le Louvre et Le Pont Caroussel, Effet de Nuit*, 1890.

CHAPTER TWO

Red velvet seats await their audience at the Opéra Garnier.

Eugène Grasset, *Théâtre National de l'Odeon*, 1890.

Chagall's mythical figures dance on the ceiling of the opera house.

The magical mirrored hall of the Grévin waxworks museum, once a theatre.

A pensive face, half drawing, half sculpture, in the garden of the Musée Zadkine, where the Russian émigré artist lived and worked.

Stone serenity at the Musée Nationale Picasso.

Brass instruments silenced in a work by Thomas Schutter, from the permanent collection of the Musée d'Art Moderne de la Ville de Paris.

Klezmer musicians entertain on the streets of the Marais.

Keeping the right profile on the streets: young...

...and old.

Stylized lovers in the garden of the Musée Zadkine recall African sculpture.

The Romanian sculptor Constantine Brancusi created his own cubist epitaph, *The Kiss*, which can be seen in the Cimetière du Montparnasse.

Expressive hands in the sculpture gallery of the Comédie Française theatre.

Ivorian dancer Georges Momboye expresses the gift of life at his African dance school, the Centre Momboye, in multiracial Ménilmontant..

The athlectic form of a 1930s bather adorns the Palais de Chaillot, built for the 1937 Exposition Internationale des Arts et des Techniques.

The Piscine Pontoise, constructed in 1933 by L. Pollet, is surrounded by individual blue and white cabins. The pool starred in the Kieslowski film *Three Colours: Blue*.

Shooting on the streets of Paris rather than in a studio, as in this scene from *Le Signe du Lion* shows, exemplified the pioneering spirit of the Nouvelle Vague.

The Grand Rex cinema, Art Deco temple to the '*septième art*'. The cinema, which in its early years had its own chorus girls and a cathedral-sized organ that rose up from the floor, was the brainchild of Jacques Haik, who also introduced Charlie Chaplin to Paris.

CHAPTER THREE

In their 19th-century heydays, *Grands Magasins* such as Bon Marché were as much a parade ground for the fashionable bourgeoisie as a retail source (unattributed engraving in *L'Illustration*).

The marché aux puces fills place d'Aligre with everything from old army uniforms to candlesticks on Tuesday to Sunday mornings. Its origins go back before the Revolution.

New trainers on the feet of a young vendor of old shoes at Montreuil.

Zen and the art of window dressing in a tiny flower shop in rue Saint-Sabin demonstrates a highly aesthetic approach to floristry.

The most famous name in French fashion can always be spotted on avenue Montaigne.

Editions de Parfums Frédéric Malle pares down scent to eight olfactory creations displayed in a minimalist showroom.

Oblivious to the roaring traffic and frequent political demonstrations, cherubs read a story on a statue at place de la République.

Enough reading matter for more than a lifetime at Librairie Ulysse on the Île St-Louis.

The rooftop of Félix Potin at 140 rue de Rennes near Montparnasse. Built in 1904 by Paul Auscher, the once sumptuous *Grand Magasin* is now a fashion boutique.

Less is more in the hi-tech but provocative display at Rodolphe Menudier shoe shop, created by über-designers the Bouroullec brothers.

Chocolate heaven at Deybauve & Gallais. The St-Germain shop once sold chocolate for medicinal purposes.

A cinderella slipper in the window of a chic vintage clothes address, Didier Ludot.

Flashback to the 60s at the perennial fashion boutique Courrèges in the smart 8th arrondissement's rue François 1er.

Paris chic doesn't rub off on all its visitors: tourists turn the camera on themselves on avenue Winston Churchill.

Parfums Caron's perfume samovars, unchanged since the 1920s and filled with re-editions of its original scents from 1911-1954.

Petits gourmands size up the sweet market, at A la Mère de Famille on rue du Fbg-Montmartre in the 9th.

The serious business of cloth at the specialist Marché St Pierre.

Paris last remaining hand wood-turner, Gérard Brucato, in his workshop in the Faubourg St -Antoine.

Salles de Bains Rétro on rue des Dames in the Batignolles neighbourhood has the last word in elegant plumbing.

Behind every great omelette there's a great *poêle*, to be found at Les Halles cooks' emporium E. Déhillerin.

A la recherche de temps perdu... clockfaces from another era among the offerings at the Marché aux Puces de St-Ouen (Clignancourt).

CHAPTER FOUR

Au Vieux Colombier, near St-Sulpice, is the very picture of a Parisian café with its green art nouveau windowframes, tightly packed tiny tables and wicker chairs.

Parisiennes practice the pout over lunch in a chic restaurant.

Recalling the grand age of train travel, art nouveau luxe at Montparnasse's Bistro de la Gare.

Late-night terrace life with a jumble of bicycles crowding the pavemen in front of Marais café l'Etoile Manquante.

Waiters outnumber customers during a quiet moment at Café Marly in the cloisters of the Louvre.

Curtain up at Le Train Blue in Gare de Lyon, one of the city's most splendid turn-of-the-20th-century brasseries.

Chef Guy Martin of Le Grand Véfour checks all is well with today's sauce.

Le Grand Véfour's dining room in the cloisters of the Palais-Royal awaits its customers. The restaurant has been operating since the 1780s and once hosted Napoléon.

A handy-shaped loaf for two-wheeled transport (and has the owner taken a bite out to sustain him on his journey?).

Time is measured out in coffee spoons.

Tarts in a pâtisserie window that are but an excuse for a fruit-fest.

At luxury épicerie Fauchon on place de la Madeleine the crystallized fruit is almost too good to eat.

While some are starchly traditional, futuristic interior design has taken hold on the the Paris restaurant scene.

The French have taken to tea connoisseurship with the seriousness that they appy to wine. Hippolyte et Romain's Japanese tea room is one of a handful where you can sample a range of rare Oriental leaves.

The Bogart era is alive and well in a timeless Parisian bistro.

Colette's minimalist water bar and restaurant refreshes the concept-store's style-conscious shoppers with its mind-boggling array of mineral waters.

As couscous is now officially the French national dish, so mint tea is becoming its second beverage of choice, served from a great height in frosted Moroccan glasses.

Variety is the spice of life at Israël delicatessen in the Marais...

CHAPTER FIVE

Bastille Day fireworks light up the Trocadéro with their annual display.

Valentino's haute couture collection comes gift-wrapped.

Early 20th century tennis at Roland Garros.

The Paris marathon sets off from the Champs-Elysées.

Déjeuner sur l'herbe on a grand scale at the Millennium picnic, seen here at parc Montsouris in the 14th.

Free open-air cinema at the parc de La Villette is a summer treat for those who choose to stay in Paris.

In winter the Parvis de l'Hôtel de Ville is turned into an ice rink.

The Pont-Neuf dressed in flowers by Kenzo, 1994...

Pastis, the aniseed drink that travelled north from Marseilles, has long been a favourite apéritif, and many cafés still serve it in the classic Art Deco named glasses.

... crammed with exotic delights from as far afield as Central Europe, the Middle East and South America.

Performers play with fire on the streets of St-Germain during the annual free music festival Fête de la Musique on midsummer's night.

Talking hats at the Prix de Diane Hermès, one of the premier race meetings of the year at Chantilly.

A carefree couple plays tennis on a traffic-free place de la Concorde in 1934.

Military pomp gets an airing at the Bastille Day parade.

High society dines in the foyer of the Opéra Garnier to celebrate a Grand Gala Performance by Maria Callas.

Opera-goers, in all their finery, gather in the foyer before a performance at the Opéra Garnier.

... and famously wrapped by the American artist Cristo in 1985.

150,000 artificial blooms filled the forecourt of The Pompidou Centre for the launch of a Kenzo perfume in 2001.

Harvest time at the Arc de Triomphe, a surreal statement organised by the ever-inventive Mairie de Paris.

Trapeze artists high in the sky at the Cirque d'Hiver winter circus, which was the setting of the film *Trapeze*. The city welcomes everything from traditional high-wire to avant-garde circus troupes.

Detail from Georges Seurat's *The Circus*, 1891.

CHAPTER SIX

Sunset over the rooftops of working-class northern Paris.

Summer nights attract picnickers and lovers to the *quai* on the Île de la Cité.

Traffic streams on the Champs-Elysées at night. In the distance Notre-Dame can just be seen.

Jenny Holzer's dramatic light projection transormed the Hôtel de Ville into a work of art for the Festival d'Automne, 2001.

A fairytale moon over the 90m medieval spire of Notre-Dame that rises far above above its square towers.

Bastille bar crawl rue de Lappe, one of the most bustling night-time haunts.

Montmartre – still the most romantic quarter of the city.

Drinking and surfing at the Web Bar, a multidisciplinary art space on the edge of the Marais. Outside is an astroturf lawn.

With its wrought-iron balconies designed by the Eiffel studio, Barrio Latino is a cocktail bar and restaurant that turns into a lively salsa club by night.

Jazz queen Josephine Baker gives it the altogether-now.

Backstage today at the Moulin Rouge.

The Art Deco façade of the Folies Bergère, which has returned to its cabaret origins.

The Elysée Montmartre, one of the great cabaret dance halls at the time of Toulouse-Lautrec, is now a concert venue and nightclub.

Hedonistic nights...

... at the Queen nightclub on the Champs-Elysées.

French manicure, Latin rhythm: dancers *merenge* at Pachanga Latin club near Montparnasse.

CHAPTER SEVEN

Glistening in the rain, Eiffel's masterpiece shows its lace tracery.

A gilded goddess stands sentinel, one of a series by different sculptors that line the central forecourt of the Palais de Chaillot.

Aptly situated on the Champ de Mars, Clara Halter's *Mur pour la Paix* speaks its message in 32 languages and 14 alphabets. Visitors are invited to add their own messages of peace via computer screens.

Ebulient breakdancers give it their all in front of the Palais de Chaillot, causing people, for once, to turn their backs on the Eiffel Tower.

Purity of form in 2.5 million rivets: note the lyre designs of the Tower's arches.

Midsummer madness on the *toits de Paris*.

The music goes on even when the shutters are down at a Bastille bar.

Moonlight and streetlamps on the Pont Alexandre III, the flamboyant bridge that links Invalides to the Grand Palais.

Millennium fireworks clothe the Eiffel Tower in glorious light.

An amusing, anthropomorphic tribute to Eiffel in the Jardin des Plantes.

Acrobats in the 1930s give the avenue de New York the atmosphere of a provincial seaside resort.

An oh-so-Parisian tribute from Jean-Paul Gaultier.

ACKNOWLEDGEMENTS

PHOTOGRAPHIC CREDITS

All photography by Jonathan Perugia,
unless credited below.

FRONTMATTER
Endpapers: © Agence VU/Bernard
Descamps
Pages 1, 2-3: © Sipa Press/Rex
Features
6-7: © Corbis/Archivo Iconografico, S.A.
8-9: © Corbis/Yann Arthus-Bertrand

INTRODUCTION
41: © Agence VU/Bertrand Desprez

CHAPTER ONE
67, 71: © Karl Blackwell
76: © Bridgeman Art Library
78-79: © AKG, London/Walter
F. Brown Collection

CHAPTER TWO
93: © Musée des Arts décoratifs,
Paris/Laurent Sully Jaulmes
96, 103: © Karl Blackwell
108-109: © Les Cahiers du
Cinema, Paris

CHAPTER THREE
124: © Mary Evans Picture Library
125, 140, 141: © Karl Blackwell

CHAPTER FOUR
160, 169: © Karl Blackwell
171: © Gilles de Chabaneix
172, 173: © Colm Pierce

CHAPTER FIVE
190, 192, 196, 197, 198, 200, 201,
204, 205, 206, 207, 208:
© Sipa Press/Rex Features
191: © David Henry
193, 202-203: © Karl Blackwell
194, 195, 199: © Keystone/Katz
209: © Corbis/Francis G. Mayer/
Edimédia

CHAPTER SIX
234: © Corbis/Bettmann
235: © Sophie Brandstrom/
L'Oeil Public
237: © Karl Blackwell

CHAPTER SEVEN
257, 263: © Sipa Press/Rex Features
261: © Keystone/Katz
264-265: © Imagebank/Getty Images

COVER
Front Cover: Jonathan Perugia

AUTHOR'S ACKNOWLEDGEMENTS

Many thanks to my colleagues at
Time Out Paris, and especially to
Rosa Jackson, and to my parents.

PUBLISHERS' ACKNOWLEDGEMENTS

The publishers would like to thank
all contributors to this title, not only
for their published material but for
all their background efforts in trying
to capture the qualities of Paris on
paper. Additional mentions go to
Elizabeth Stone, Karl Blackwell
(www.karlblackwellphoto.co.uk)
and Pippa Isbell.

For more information on
Orient-Express services, visit
www.orient-express.com

First published in Great Britain
in 2003 by
PAVILION BOOKS LTD

An imprint of Chrysalis Books Group plc

The Chrysalis Building
Bramley Road
London W10 6SP
www.chrysalisbooks.co.uk

ISBN 1 86205 517 3

Design/layout © Pavilion Books, 2003
Text © Pavilion Books, 2003
Photographs © Pavilion Books, 2003,
except where credited otherwise

Series concept: Sandra Harris
Designer: Stafford Cliff
Editor: Emily Preece-Morrison
Photographer: Jonathan Perugia
(achildseye@yahoo.com)
Picture research: Corine Thuilier-
Delahaie
Production artwork: Ian Hammond
Publisher: Vivien James

Printed by: Leefung-Asco Printers
Holdings Ltd., China